Sharon Blain

THE CONFIDENT STYLIST

First Published in 2023 by Echo Books

Echo Books is an imprint of Superscript Publishing Pty Ltd
ABN 76 644 812 395

Registered Office: PO Box 997, Woodend, Victoria, 3442

www.echobooks.com.au

Copyright © Sharon Blain

National Library of Australia Cataloguing-in-Publication entry.

Creator: Blain, Sharon, author.

Title: The Confident Stylist: Sharon Blain

ISBN: 978-1-922603-79-1 (paperback)

A catalogue record for this book is available from the National Library of Australia

Book and cover design by Andrew Davies.

Contents

Introduction		7
Chapter 1	The fundamentals of design	11
Chapter 2	Face and body shapes	33
Chapter 3	Hair characteristics	53
Chapter 4	Styling tools audit	67
Chapter 5	Styling products	83
Chapter 6	Braids	91
Chapter 7	Curl science and theory	101
Chapter 8	Blow-drying	111
Chapter 9	Waves	121
Chapter 10	Thermal setting	131
Chapter 11	Styling hacks	141
Chapter 12	Fashion and history	163
Chapter 13	Thought provoking avant-garde	175
Chapter 14	The creative process	193
Chapter 15	Material list and budget	201
Chapter 16	My Renaissance Collection	215
Appendix	Image Credits	222
	Acknowledgements	225

INTRODUCTION

THE CONFIDENT STYLIST has been written with you in mind... and I've poured my passion for hair into every word! During my long and successful career in the hair industry, I've gathered 50+ years of knowledge and wisdom that you'll now find in these pages.

It's part textbook, part life experience, part thought-provoking, and part extraordinary must-have information that's designed to elevate you to THE CONFIDENT STYLIST I know you can be.

Hands up if you've spent hours scouring the internet or Googling information in search of the finer points of how to execute beautifully dressed hair? Your search is over, because THE CONFIDENT STYLIST is the most comprehensive styling guide out there.

I've covered in detail how *'old school'* techniques establish the basis for many of today's hair trends, and why this knowledge forms the essential foundations of your styling success. You'll be far more confident when creating timeless hair using proven techniques that continue to stand the test of time.

I want you to fully understand how perfecting these skills will open the door to a broader range of styling options, and importantly, styling confidence. Developing your understanding of this essential knowledge will, over time, become part of your styling DNA. And in turn you'll finally expand your artistic expertise and become a true master of your craft.

As you immerse yourself in the information covered throughout this guide, you'll soon learn how my simplified version of the design elements correlates perfectly to styling hair. And I'll also share why it's important to understand the role shape, form, and design play on your path to styling excellence. Additionally, numerous chapters will cover the theory on setting, waves, and blow-drying, plus the impact of face and body shapes.

Nothing has been left out – and the information will challenge your artistic thought process, leaving you with many *Aha!* moments.

I'll also go into the impact fashion has had throughout the decades, and how history continues to inspire and influence the evolution of contemporary hair styling today.

Storytelling is part of everyday life, and this guide is crafted to help stylists and lovers of hair understand the relationship between storytelling and creating a visual storyboard when designing hair for editorial or hair collections. I've got you covered if you've ever wondered where to start, where to find inspiration, how to plan, and how to ensure you follow through and execute your finished masterpiece.

The detailed information you're about to dive into is priceless and hard to find elsewhere – it will quickly become the only styling bible you'll ever need!

And don't worry, I haven't overlooked the topic I get asked about all the time! These pages are jam-packed with in-depth information about the different hair styling tools currently available and my favourite 'hot' must-haves! Have you ever wondered what hot tool to select for different looks and the different results they deliver? Check out the chapter dedicated to this – it will take away the mystery and guesswork, because I've done all the research and had the epic fails on your behalf!

I couldn't resist adding a few extra chapters at the end about my favourite topic, avant-garde styling. I know you'll love the list of all the materials, glues, wigs, and craft items I use to create my pieces. I'll let you in on how my iconic Renaissance Collection evolved and get you thinking about your own creative path.

Want more? A regular topic amongst hairdressers is what hair products they like to use and their favourite brands. I decided to add a full chapter on what styling products are essential for creating fabulous hair, breaking down each one and when to use them.

Naturally, I've shared my top secrets when it comes to my favourite products. And as a special little bonus, you'll find my much-loved hair hack that's like gold in your hands! It will definitely come in handy when a magical hair day is in order.

So here we go!

As a global master stylist, I've done the legwork for you over the past 5 decades, and I've poured my love and passion for hair into this styling bible. I'm so honoured and excited to see where this information takes *you*!

Strap yourself in, your styling journey is about to take off...

CHAPTER 1

THE FUNDAMENTALS OF DESIGN

'Harmony is the ability to create a feeling of tranquillity, peace and beauty.'

– SHARON BLAIN

Like me, you may not at first grasp the importance of why the fundamentals of design are key to creating stunning hairstyles. Let me assure you, once you understand the concept, and the reasons why they exist, your styling and creativity will begin to flourish.

The meaning of **design**: To create or construct according to plan.

The meaning of **fundamental**: A primary rule or principle on which something is based.

The **fundamentals of design**: The foundation of every visual design, and the practical success of the design.

We often speak about how influential fashion designers and iconic hairstylists have a 'great eye for design' – and this is usually because they intuitively know what works best. Their choice of design, fabric, style, and textures invariably leads to winning results.

The iconic hairstylist knows what suits a body or face shape, the best colours to put together, or how to combine different textures and patterns, and they are the masters at creating that wow factor. These masters truly understand the basic fundamentals of design.

As time evolves, your techniques will improve, your skill set will keep developing, and your enquiring mind will open a Pandora's box of creativity. You'll begin to explore, challenging yourself and experimenting with different ways to create. Your eyes will become trained, and your awareness will be heightened with a keen understanding as to why your creation is fantastic or a flop.

It's then that you'll begin designing hairstyling masterpieces, and over time you'll become more intuitive with the creative process. So much of this process is due to having a deeper understanding of the theory of design.

Over the years, I did struggle to see the relationship between the theory of design and how it worked with hair. I've come to realise that it was due to lack of available information.

When researching the fundamentals of design, I found such a vast amount of varying information online. And I found it difficult to comprehend or even break down how this type of information related to styling hair.

It's important to mention here that the fundamentals of design are generic and apply to all forms of design – be it fashion, floristry, architecture, graphic design, photography, hair styling, and so on.

Floral design is a hobby of mine, and I spent many years learning and finessing my skills. It was during this learning period that I was able to see the comparison between flower arrangements and hair design. I came to understand that both rely on the same fundamental design principles – for example, when arranging a flower bouquet, my visual observations include shape and design as well as playing with space in a 3D view. This also applies when I'm designing a hairstyle.

Learning these principles through a creative pursuit other than hairstyling has allowed me to develop a deeper understanding of the fundamentals of design.

I believe there are ten key design fundamentals that best translate to styling hair, and these have made a huge difference to my success as a stylist. I want to stress that they are essential to understand, and I recommend you study them in great depth, as they will help you go a long way in perfecting your craft.

Learn them, love them, and practice them!

Then in time, at just a glance, you'll intuitively be able see what will work and what won't when examining any hairstyle.

Below you'll find an overview of each of the fundamentals of design, their meaning, and a brief correlation of their relationship to hair design.

10 KEY FUNDAMENTALS OF DESIGN

1 Shape and form

The **shape** is the outline shape of the design, while the form plays with the space it occupies within the design. Shape can be either organic, geometric, symmetrical, or asymmetrical, and is also described as two-dimensional. 2D means that what you see is flat in appearance, with only the two dimensions of length and width – this is exactly the shape you see when you look at a sketch or a drawing.

In comparison, form is referred to as three-dimensional because it comprises the length, width, depth, and the volume. To help grasp the difference between form and shape, imagine a flat circle is the shape, while a 3D sphere is the form.

Organic form is free-flowing like shapes found in nature. Think plants, flowers, and branches which have no hard edges and are usually not a definitive shape.

In comparison, geometric shapes are very easy to identify and label. These are shapes such as a circle, square, rectangle, oval, and so on.

2 Line

This is all about which direction the line of the design takes the eye, defining form and space. **Line** is used to define the outline of the shapes within a hair design. These lines can be vertical or horizontal, curved or diagonal, contrasting or transitional.

In hair design we create an optical illusion with lines – I like to think about lines as a way to draw around the edge of a style. If it's a bob for example, the line would be drawn horizontally around the edge of the bob. The directions of a line in hair design can give the illusion of the style being longer, shorter, or wider, and the line can also direct the eye to a specific feature of the design or focal point.

Curved lines soften the edges of a design, giving a more organic movement. Horizontal lines that run across the bottom of a design give the illusion of width. Vertical lines add the illusion of height. Diagonal forward lines direct the eye towards the face, and diagonal back lines lead the eye towards the back. Lines that run both vertical and horizontal add the illusion of width and height.

3 Colour

Colour plays a large part in design. Knowing how colour plays with light, resulting in reflection or absorption of light on the surface, is essential to good design and gaining the outcome you desire. We know some hair colour pigments will reflect light, while others absorb the light.

Let's take for example white or lighter blonde hair colour, it visually appears alive and bright, and has the ability to reflect various colour hues and light.

Black or darker hair colour, however, has the highest absorption of light, with very little light reflected off it, which is why visually it will appear dark or heavy.

When photographing hair, it's important to remember that the colour tones of the hair can vary depending on the different types of lighting used and its brightness.

Colour will always enhance a hair design, and it tends to bring a hairstyle to life by adding an extra dimension to the finished look. It's the difference between bland, beige, or breathtakingly brilliant.

The image above shows a wig that was one solid shade of white with special cutting lines. Definition was needed to accentuate the lines so they would be visible in a photograph. In order to achieve this, grey colour was added along the edges to create depth and contrast and overall the image looks far more dramatic by doing so.

Never before has colour been so popular, especially if you look at social media. Colour plays such a huge role in salon services and is becoming the most requested salon service today.

It's super important to understand the role colour plays and the different effects colour has when styling hair. For example, imagine a beautiful blonde hair model with stunning classic Hollywood waves, great facial features, and perfectly executed showstopper waves.

Now imagine the same model and same Hollywood waves with dark brown hair – it still looks great, but it just misses the mark (apart from the perfect styling and finish) because it's often the colour that brings a style to life. The detail of the Hollywood wave movement can be lost in a darker hair colour. Remember when working with darker hair shades, less hair detail will be apparent.

Light also plays a role with hair colour and how it affects and interacts with the different levels of colour. With lighter blonde tones, the light reflecting off the hair will appear bigger and fuller. With darker hair tones, the light is absorbed, creating the illusion of being smaller and appearing shinier and smoother to the eye. Again, the peaks and troughs of a wave movement are more obvious with lighter hair.

Here are two images as a visual comparison between a light and dark hair colouring with a similar hairstyle – have a look at the different effect created by the varying depth of colour.

4 Texture

Texture is the visual appearance of the hair surface and how the hair looks and feels – it can be curly, wavy, kinky, straight, smooth, or frizzy.

The image to the right shows two distinct textures – smooth and activated. Note the smooth texture on the top, which looks more polished and shows definite details. Whereas the pony texture is airy and soft. This texture lacks any form of detail or polish due to the deconstructed nature of the texture.

When texture is added to a hairstyle, it adds a different dimension to the overall look. Texture can give the hair a more casual lived-in appearance, or it can be used to create a massive avant-garde style. Often a combination of different types of textures are used within a style. For example, adding voluminous curls by crimping the roots creates texture and volume at the roots, and soft feminine curls on the ends. On the other hand, smooth hair surfaces will give a more polished classic finish and can make the hair appear smaller on the head.

I also want to explain the meaning of deactivated and activated texture: Naturally curly hair is described as having activated texture, and the same can be said for hair that has frizz, body, and bounce. Deactivated texture is smooth, flat, straight hair, that lays flat without any movement.

Slow and fast movement also relates to texture – a very gentle wave movement is considered as having slow movement, whilst a strong frizzy movement is known as being fast. To help understand how this information works technically in hair styling, a look could be described as having activated texture with fast movement.

5 Balance and harmony

Balance can be symmetrical or asymmetrical within a design. Both symmetrical and asymmetrical balance are used extensively in hair designs and cutting.

Symmetrical shape: Both sides are identical, as they are a mirror image of each other.

Asymmetrical shape: Each half is different, or one side is more dramatic, but it's still visually pleasing to the eye with a balanced proportion.

The image to the left shows a great visual of the meaning of symmetry and balance. The size of the chignon shape shows good overall balance in relationship to the position where it sits on the head. The chignon is also the perfect size for the scalp space. This is a great example of balance and harmony, and also very pleasing to the eye.

Harmony is achieved when all the elements work harmoniously together. When our eyes see harmony, a feeling of peace and tranquillity prevails. The goal of any stylist is to create a stunning masterpiece of which to be proud. Developing an eye for recognising good balance and harmony takes time and practice, but is worth it as it creates unity within the overall design.

I consider harmony the most important principle to understand. To achieve the ideal balance, the model's features must be taken into consideration. Firstly, a good consultation is of the greatest importance and necessary to establish the preferred hairstyle. Always paying attention to the face shape, head shape, body, neck, and facial profile helps to achieve good balance.

To achieve perfect harmony, all the elements must work well together, namely the texture, balance, colour, shape, and form. Harmony creates a feeling of tranquillity, peace, and beauty. Harmony delivers an overall appreciation of the hairstyle, and a sense of satisfaction.

6 Discord

Discord is the opposite of harmony, and a lot of stylists create it without realising. It's when clashing textures, a bad mix of colour tones, or a mismatch of braids are used in an odd way with no consideration for balance or harmony. The result is too many different types of braids and frizz all fighting it out within the design.

It's what I would describe as a 'hot mess'. Just because you can, doesn't mean you should! As a reference, explore the admired Antoni Gaudi, the famous Spanish architect. His work is highly individualistic and modernistic. Discord plays a part in his designs – his work is thought provoking and controversial, but very much admired. He was able to use discord within the parameters of good design and he knew how far to go and where to stop.

The image I've included above could be considered controversial. It's open to discussion as to whether the lack of conformity and clashing of design fits within the design elements. Discord is usually left of centre and non-conventional, but it can still be admired due to the uniqueness of the design.

7 Proportion

This is the relationship between the size of the design and how well it plays with the space. **Proportion** is very similar to balance – however, there are some key differences. While balance is the placement of the hair within the design, proportion is the relationship between the size of the hair design in relation to the overall face and body frame. *The above image shows a great balance between the height, width, face shape, and head size.*

As an example, adding a small tight top knot on a super tall, larger framed woman, could be seen as the hairstyle being too small and out of proportion for the large body frame. Now add the same top knot on a small petite body shape, and the proportion sits perfectly and in total harmony with the facial features and body frame.

8 Focal point

This is the point of the design to where the eye is drawn. Have you heard the phrase called the 'money piece' when colouring hair? Basically, it's an area that has been coloured in a special way to make the features pop! It's also known as the **focal point**. *The focal point in the style pictured above is the unique placement of the combs. Your eye is immediately drawn to the combs, then to the overall design.*

To grasp this further, imagine a bowl of green apples with a red apple in the middle. If you guessed that the red apple is the focal point, you're correct! Now picture a sleek classic chignon at the nape - the focal point of this style is the chignon, and your eye is drawn to the chignon shape. That one focal point could be a stunning wave movement, a cute top knot, or a power pony. It's important to keep the area surrounding the focal point simple in its design.

Never be tempted to add too many different frizzy textures, waves, or braids into a top knot all together in the one hair design. It's distracting to the eye and shows poor design skills. Avoid overkill and don't add more than one focal point. Knowing when to stop is an art. Keeping your design simple is the key to good styling.

9 Repetition

This is about regularly repeating the same design in a predictable way, or an element within a design that continually repeats itself. A flat zig-zag set is the best example of **repetition**. Also consider the three-strand braid or a classic woven highlight – the repetition in these examples is continuous, creating a pattern. In relation to hair, think of an alternating small and large tong set vertically around the head as repetition. *The picture above demonstrates the repetitive pattern braiding creates.*

10 Rhythm

Rhythm is created when a design is repeated with variation. I think the best way to understand *rhythm* is to look at animal print patterned fabric. You generally see different squiggly pattern shapes with a variety of sizes and colour tones repeating itself throughout the design. *In the image to the left, the eyes are drawn to the wave, that shows variation of the waves size and depth and the direction it travels.*

The same can be said when looking at a 3D finger wave pattern that has peaks and troughs and continues to follow the same pattern from roots to ends.

The diagram below is a visual example of a collection of the fundamentals we've just covered.

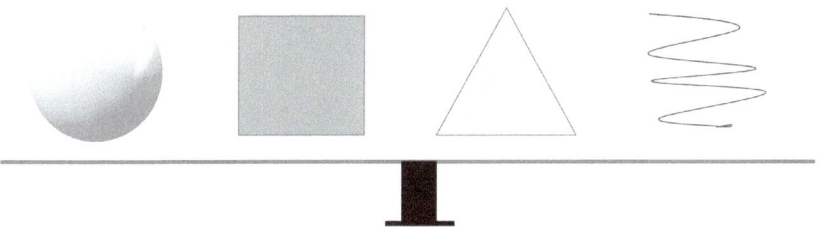

The sphere represents shape and form, creating depth and playing with the space around it. The square represents a 2D shape which is the overall outline of the design, the triangle is also a 2D shape with texture and colour, and the squiggly line represents hair texture, while the line underneath shows hair direction. By combining these symbols together, you'll have all the elements of good design and balance essential for styling beautiful hair.

Here are some practical tips using the fundamentals of design:

A practical step and simple rule I teach in every class is easy to visualise and will help you develop the perfect balance and shape. Consider the triangle shape, which is the easiest of shapes to recognise when creating an updo. Although there are many different shapes that can work successfully, the triangle is a simple shape that works with most face shapes.

I recommend standing back from your work during the dressing out process, as it's essential to observe how the shape of the style is developing. Make sure you look at the entire head – the front, back and side profile, to ensure the balance and shape is working for the wearer.

This way, you are developing your eye for shape, and your eye will be easily trained. Especially when seeking out a simple triangle shape within your design. I'd also suggest having your phone handy to take shots of all the angles to see any imperfections that need to be adjusted to perfect the shape.

You should now have a better understanding of the importance of the fundamentals of design and how they play an intricate part in the design process.

This may be the first time you've heard about the fundamentals, but I can assure you, if you were a student of fashion, interior design, or graphic design, this information would be included as part of the curriculum. It is included in the hairdressing curriculum, but perhaps a little more detail is required to get the full understanding of its importance and relevance.

I've tried to keep the information simple and easy to comprehend and I encourage you to explore this information on a more advanced level in your downtime. It's a fascinating journey that has no boundaries.

I always felt I was doing great hair until delving deeper into this subject. It has helped me enormously to see hair in a different way and helped me create better hair collections.

Without this necessary information, your best intentions and inspirations can fall short, and you may continue to struggle to execute excellent designs.

The design relationship I found between floral arrangements and hairstyling

To give a more visual understanding between the relationship of floristry to hair, I've included some interesting visual examples for you to see how hair styling and flower designs can crossover.

In two of the *floral designs pictured to the right*, the presence of a triangle shape has been created by the way the leaves around the outline have been placed. I love the contemporary and very individual nature of these arrangements.

The same can be said for the hair images.

Although these looks are considered free-flowing and avant-garde, it's still possible to see **round, triangle** and **asymmetric** shapes within them.

The biggest message I want to share here is that you should always try to work with a definite shape in mind when styling hair. When looking for great inspiration, it's hard to go past a beautiful floral design to bring your masterpiece to life!

Asymmetrical

Triangular

Round

CHAPTER 2

FACE AND BODY SHAPES

'Learn the rules like a Pro,

so you can break them like an Artist.'

– PABLO PICASSO

The next step to being a confident stylist is to look at face and body shapes in greater detail.

I touched on face shapes briefly in the previous chapter, in reference to the fundamentals of shape and form, and the importance of analysing the face from a 3D perspective. This requires observing the structure of the face, side profile, scalp, size, and shape, as well as the length and size of the neck and the person's height and body proportion. Essentially it is observing the shape and form.

Firstly, never use a cape to cover the body when doing the analysis, it's important to observe the entire body from top to toe. It's impossible to conduct a detailed analysis when the neck, shoulders, and body are covered.

I can't impress upon you enough the importance of assessing face and body shape in detail. This type of assessment will aid in the perfect style choice for your client. Without appearing to be tactless, you must consider the additional points I've detailed on the following page. Overlooking these points will result in disappointment at the end.

For example, I always make a point of double checking the ears. This became a must, especially after I once booked a model for a hair shoot who had very obvious protruding ears. The entire day was spent trying to tape her ears back to her head, not an easy job, and quite painful I may add. This was in the era when Photoshop wasn't yet an option to make these kinds of adjustments. Believe me, it's never happened again! And as for those protruding ears, think voluminous curls as a possible solution.

There are six different face shapes: **oval, heart, round, square, oblong** and **diamond**. The oval face shape is my preferred choice. With this shape there are no limits styling wise.

On the following pages I've included a set of guidelines to help identify the various face shapes, which will make your styling selections easier and enhance the wearer's features. There are groups of styles that work best with certain face shapes and it's advisable to not only understand them in great detail, but also learn how to tweak each look to suit different faces.

As fashion trends come and go, it's vital to note here that just because it's in fashion doesn't mean it's going to suit everyone. Having a professional consultation with your client and pointing out the best options for their features will help grow a long loyal fan base and a happy client.

OVAL

The above style is a great example of how to frame an oval face shape.

Oval shape

Has a symmetrical shape, with the forehead and jawline approximately the same width. Providing the face is in proportion, most sleek or soft texture styles will suit an oval face shape – think *Jessica Alba*.

Oval Style Guide – Long sleek bobs, soft textured nape or crown buns, fringes, centre parting classic 1940s inspired waves.

HEART

The added fullness on the crown in the image above is a perfect style for a heart face shape.

Heart shape

Will be wider at the forehead with prominent cheekbones that taper into a soft pointy chin. Some heart-shaped faces also have a defined widow's peak in the centre of the forehead – think *Reese Witherspoon*.

Heart Style Guide – Soft crown curls, side parting, long side swept fringe, soft down waves, hair half up and half down, loose ponytails.

ROUND

The asymmetrical hair design in this image complements a round face shape perfectly.

Round shape

Has a broader, rounder shape compared to the oval shape – with the length and width generally equal. The round edges are softer with the widest point at the cheekbone – think *Kelly Osbourne*.

Round Style Guide – Asymmetrical styles, top knots, sleek lobs, shaggy textured looks, face framing pieces.

SQUARE

The beautiful style above is designed to flatter a square face shape.

Square shape

Forehead, cheekbones and jawline are the same width. Generally, the strong square jawline is the most prominent feature – think *Angelina Jolie*.

Square Style Guide – Dramatic side parting, root volume texture, side sweeping waves, curls or textured braids, soft nape shapes, with face framing pieces.

OBLONG

Like in the image above, a combination of twisted draped hair and face tendrils will complement an oblong face shape.

Oblong shape

An elongated rectangle in shape – the forehead, cheekbones and jawline are in an elongated line without width or narrow areas. Some have prominent chins – think *Alexa Chung*.

Oblong Style Guide – Soft relaxed face framing movement, centre parting ponytail, curtain fringes, classic side swept curls.

DIAMOND

The above timeless half-up half-down hairstyle complements various face shapes, and is especially suited to a diamond shape.

Diamond shape

Has similarities to the heart shape. However, the cheekbones are generally higher, along with a narrower forehead. The chin area has a soft pointy chin – think *Jennifer Lopez*.

Diamond Style Guide – Soft dishevelled up-styles, volume crown buns, power ponytail, voluminous curls and waves, hair tucked behind the ears, straight fringes.

FACE PROFILES

Having established the various face shapes, the next step is to consider face profiles. It's important to assess the client's profile, looking from the side of the face.

There are three profiles: **flat, convex** and **concave**.

While analysing the profile, also take note of the head or skull shape. It may be perfect in proportion, round, flat at the crown, or bumpy with odd dips. By running your hands over the skull, it's easy to feel any imperfections – and this is important to consider when designing the style.

Using a mirror when doing this will help give a better overall view of the client's features. Moving the hair around the face and in various directions will also help establish what shape and style will suit.

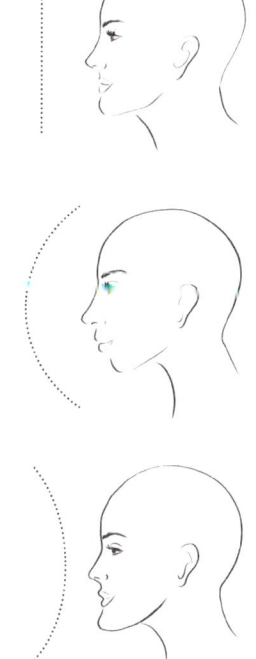

Flat or straight profile

No protruding or prominent features, making it easy to create any requests for a hairstyle.

Convex profile

Generally, has a sloping receding chin and forehead angle. This forces the nose to be the most prominent feature.

Concave profile

This is where the forehead and chin protrude forward which gives the area around the nose and mouth a more convex position.

Now let's go a step further to tie all this information together.

I've created a special checklist below with points to double check in order to avoid ending up with a 'protruding ears' style scenario:

- **Neck**: Short, long, thin, or thick
- **Forehead**: Wide, narrow, high or low
- **Nose**: Pointy and/or hooked, convex in profile, or caved, creating a concave profile
- **Ears**: Protruding or flat
- **Eyes**: Heavy hooded, wide, or close set
- **Chin/Jawline**: Excessively pointy and sharp, receding down into the neck, protruding out further than the forehead, pronounced sharp jawline or less obvious jawline
- **Hairline/Scalp**: Low, high or sparse with strong growth patterns that can create unbalanced hairlines

The neck – Must be considered when styling or cutting hair. You'll encounter short, long, thick, or extra-long swan-like necks. I spend a lot of time banging on about the importance of taking neck size into consideration prior to styling or cutting!

All too often we see a client whose hair has been cut way too short, especially at the nape. This can result in an unflattering look, and I can't stress enough the importance of making sure the style or cut you create is always flattering in relation to the profile of the client's face. Thicker necks and heavy jowls are difficult to disguise and do look much softer and more attractive when soft looser shapes or longer length cuts are created.

For example, for shorter, wider necks that include a double chin, the hair is best dressed softly on the lower crown, leaving a few loose tendrils at the nape which helps to direct the eye away from the neck area. Avoid shaving or tapering the neckline short, leaving it a little longer with a softer shape.

The forehead – Whilst some foreheads can be quite high or very low, others can be narrower or wider and quite prominent. It's how the hair is placed on the forehead that will help to correct or enhance. Try to bring hair down onto the face with a higher forehead, and take the hair back and away with a low hairline. When dealing with a wider hairline, correct it by adding softness at the sides of the face to narrow it. Avoid adding width to the side areas of the face.

As a quick fix for a sparse hairline, think temporary extensions, or plan a style with root texture using a volume tool like my *Elevate Pro Styler*, which will make the hair appear thicker.

The nose – From my experience, I don't believe there are too many people reading this that absolutely love their nose. Maybe those women who have paid thousands for plastic surgery are happy, but most wish their nose was more like Nicole, Kylie, or Angelina's.

As a stylist, this is where all our skills are put to the test. Especially at the consultation stage of the design process. Firstly, coming up with a great plan, and secondly trying to steer a determined person away from a desired style that will not work. Tact always plays a big role here as well.

As I write this guide, the trend at the moment is a centre parting with a 'curtain fringe'. I've got to be honest, it might be on-trend, but it certainly doesn't suit everyone. Especially not clients who have prominent noses. A centre parting can mainly be worn successfully by someone with a perfect symmetrical face shape and a perfectly proportioned nose.

Take your time and don't rush, hold the hair, and move it around the face and scalp, checking the front, side and back profiles to determine what looks best for their features and face shape. Learning to design looks that are in keeping with the latest trends, but still flatter different noses and face shapes, definitely requires a skill that takes time to master. It's such a visual thing, but as your eye for designing kicks in, the style selection process becomes simple and routine.

The ears – It's all about creating styles that flatter and bring out the best in all of us, so if you're working with protruding ears, softening the style can help. Softening options include dishevelling, loosening, and adjusting designs so that hair is sweeping across the ears. At all costs, avoid designs that are sleek and smooth, with the hair sitting behind protruding ears. The idea is to take attention away from features you don't want to highlight.

The eyes – To assess if the eyes are wide or close set, imagine a 'third eye' sitting on the bridge of the nose fitting perfectly in between the gap of both eyes. This quick test will help establish if the eyes are close or wide set. If the 'third eye' overlaps the eyes, the eyes are considered close set. If there is a space either side of the 'third eye' and the actual eyes, then the eyes are considered wide set.

With perfectly balanced eyes, any hairstyle will suit. Otherwise, various adjustments will need to be made to flatter these facial variations. With heavy hooded eyes, don't add a heavy fringe as it closes the face down – instead, move the hair back to open up the face.

The chin/jawline – If you're dealing with a double chin, a protruding, or a recessed chin, during the consultation an open discussion with your client is essential and this is where a skilled artist comes into play by camouflaging imperfections. You can't change the chin, but you can certainly create a style that draws attention away from this feature. The style created with hair will give an optical illusion, deflecting the eye away from the chin, and instead towards the stunning style. If the jawline sits outside the oval face structure and is more angular, you'll need to consider if the finished hair design should have a softer texture or finish.

The hairline/scalp – While examining the scalp for any imperfections, it's important to analyse any irregular growth patterns on the hairline, crown, and nape. Check for any sparse or balding areas and determine the density of the hair.

Note: Hair density will be covered in greater detail later in this guide.

How I like to divide the face during an analysis of proportion and face shape

To support the information in this chapter, I want to further explain how to break down a face shape on a more advanced level.

By dividing the face into smaller sections, you gain a better understanding of how to view a perfectly proportioned face. This is illustrated in the diagram below.

Vertical lines: Divide the face in 3 sections down the sides and middle of the face.

Horizontal lines: Divide the face in 3 sections across the top to the bottom of the face.

Start by running two horizontal lines across the face. One through the centre of the eyes, the second across the tip of the nose.

When measured from the hairline to the eyes to the tip of the nose, then, from the nose to the chin - the three sections should be equal in size for the perfect balance. If any section is not in proportion to another, the hair design should be adjusted to suit the face.

Running two vertical lines down the face will help you analyse if the width of the face is balanced and in equal proportion. The two lines should run through the centre of the eyes, and when measured from the hairline to the centre of the eyes on both sides, they should be of equal width.

The diagram *on the previous page* will help your understanding of what a perfectly balanced face should look like. Unfortunately, very few people fit this model, but hopefully it will help give you a greater understanding of what should be considered when designing for a person's face shape.

You've just learnt the true value of understanding face shapes and how our skills can perform magic when designing hairstyles for clients. You've also learnt to bring out the best in them, whilst minimising features when required.

BODY SHAPES

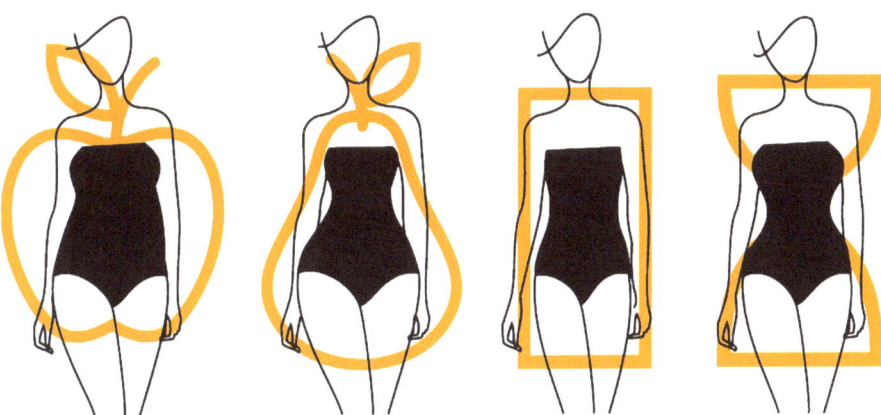

Now let's take a look at how important it is to consider body shape and how it fits into the world of hair styling. I spoke about an 'optical illusion' earlier, and how the eye can be deceived into believing something that's not actually the case. Choosing the correct style of clothing for different body styles also gives an optical illusion.

The right cut dress can make a bigger body appear smaller, vertical stripes can make you look taller, horizontal lines make the body look wide, and so on. I'd encourage you to take a deep dive into the vast information available and explore the 'dos and don'ts' in relationship to body shape and clothing.

With body shapes, it's wise to better understand what suits, such as the best cuts, colours, and patterns. A great place to learn this first is on ourselves!

The main message I want to express here is the importance of the 'total look'. The body and face shape should work in unison, always complementing features to deliver that *wow* factor.

Your hair can either balance and enhance your body shape, or draw attention to a feature you may not like.

As an example, with a short petite body shape, the longer the hair is, the more the body and hair will appear out of proportion. The hair can make the body look even shorter. Alternatively, cutting the hair shorter, and styling with volume, adds height and length to the body, creating an optical illusion overall.

Another example is cutting hair way too short on a tall, larger framed, pear-shaped body. The eye will immediately be drawn to the body shape, not the great haircut. *But* if the hair was slightly longer in length, it would complement and appear in balance with the overall look, creating that optical illusion. Body shape falls into different types. Namely, rectangle, apple, hourglass, and pear or inverted triangle.

Rectangle shape: This is the most common body shape; it is uniform in measurement or straight in build. The most flattering hair for this body type is medium length with width at the sides. Consider soft curl texture.

Apple shape: The midsection and waist is fuller, commonly referred to as curvy. To balance this body type, choose a medium length hair that adds fullness and movement at the crown to give the illusion of length to the body and to balance the proportion.

Hourglass shape: Hips and bust are nearly equal in size, while the waist is narrower than both. Wearing smooth straight hair will accentuate this shape. It's best to add waves or soft texture to the hair.

Pear or inverted triangle: Generally, this body shape has larger hips in proportion to the width of the shoulders. Avoid styling the hair too close to the head as it accentuates the imbalance. Rather, create fullness to the sides and the top of the head.

PERSONALISED STYLE

I recommend doing some more research to look further into information about how *personalised style* works, and I've given you some examples of this below. It definitely helps to make client consultations easier when you understand where your client fits.

Since learning how everyone falls naturally into different 'style' categories (see examples below), my hairstyle selection has simplified, and client satisfaction has been far greater.

This is a short overview showing how the puzzle fits together with the use of personalised style categories or types:

Classic
Fashion: Timeless looks, simple elegant cuts in clothing
Hairstyle: Sleek Bobs, polished simple chignon
Think – Audrey Hepburn, Amal Clooney, and Catherine, Princess of Wales

Natural
Fashion: Casual sporty, natural fibres, relaxed jackets and draw string pants
Hairstyle: Easy care cut, dishevelled curls, messy bun
Think – Jennifer Aniston, Martha Stewart, Judi Dench

Creative
Fashion: Vintage, colourful mixed designs and avant-garde street fashion
Hairstyle: Bold colour, wild alternative cuts, and extreme styling
Think – Vivienne Westwood, Lady Gaga, Carrie Bradshaw

Romantic
Fashion: Floral, softer, longer chiffon loose flowing skirts
Hairstyle: Loose floating curls, soft tousled wavy cuts, boho braids
Think – Penelope Cruz, Taylor Swift, Keira Knightley

'If knowledge is a power,

then learning is a superpower.'

– JIM KWIK,

MEMORY AND BRAIN COACH

CHAPTER 3

HAIR CHARACTERISTICS

In the following chapters you'll discover the characteristics of hair. I'll cover the role hair plays when determining a suitable style, the techniques to use, and the best products and tools needed for achieving styling perfection.

Over my 50+ years as a stylist, I've developed techniques that really work, along with products I prefer to use and ways to prepare the hair for optimal performance. I openly share this information with my students and hair community, and I'm excited to share it with you now.

Below I've outlined the hair characteristics that need to be theoretically understood and considered for achieving design success:

- Hair fibre and texture

- Hair types

- Hair elasticity

- Hair porosity

- Hair density

- Hair length

HAIR FIBRE AND TEXTURE

This considers the individual hair fibres to determine the physical properties of each fibre. The main physical properties of hair depend mostly on its geometry – for example, the shape of a Caucasian hair fibre is oval, Asian hair fibre is circular, while Afro hair fibre is a flat/oval or elliptical shape.

It's important to understand the physical inner structure of the different hair fibres and the role this plays when determining why different hair types perform so differently.

HAIR TYPES

ASIAN HAIR — Round shape follicle

AFRO-TEXTURED HAIR — Eliptical shape follicle

CAUCASIAN HAIR — Oval shape follicle

This image is a visual example of the three different hair shapes and how it grows out from the scalp.

For example, round or oval shaped hair in its original form is mouldable and has the ability to bend and bounce freely. Let's say that the hair works with you and not against you.

Here is an example to help illustrate this a little more – if you straighten hair with a straightening iron, the shape of the hair is flattened. Now this might sound a little strange, but I like to use an example of comparing straightened hair to a piece of cardboard to help better understand how the shape of flat hair fibres react when straightened.

Try rolling up a piece of cardboard into a cylinder shape, it will only remain in a cylinder shape when tied tightly together with pressure. Once released, it will spring back to its original shape in minutes. A piece of cardboard is not flexible enough to hold a different shape unless forced.

This is what happens when straightening the hair prior to setting or curling, since the straightening iron will change the internal structure to a flat pancake shape. That flat shape does not have the ability to maintain curl as well as a round or oval shape. It very quickly reverts back to the flat shape. Hence the 'cardboard' analysis.

After straightening, the flat shape temporarily limits the flexibility of the hair, and it will hang down poker straight. Tong setting on top of straightened hair won't give as long-lasting curls, which is obviously not ideal when you need to have fabulous hair with lots of body and bounce. This is the opposite situation to what you want – the hair is now working against you rather than with you.

Texture plays a huge part in the performance of the hair. When we talk about texture in relation to hair, it's the 'feel' of the hair that's important to understand when beginning any hairstyle. If you don't get it right in the beginning, it will be an uphill battle and you'll be fighting the hair all the way to achieve your visual expectations.

'Cotton not silk' is a regular phrase used to describe how the hair texture should feel. The best type of hair texture to work with when styling should feel a little rough and coarse. Compare this to a soft slippery silky hair texture, which is near impossible to work with when trying to create an up-style. For this very reason as mentioned above, it's not advisable to use a straightener anytime when preparing the hair prior to styling.

Some hair types naturally have a coarse texture. There are other hair types that develop 'cotton' like texture when the hair has been highly coloured or bleached. The reason being is that the cuticle is more open

and susceptible to damage after colouring, causing the hair to feel rougher.

Granted it's not ideal to have damaged coloured hair, but it certainly makes styling hair much easier. To achieve a 'cotton' like hair texture when working with super fine soft hair, or chemically untreated hair, it's all about layering products during the preparation stage. I'll go into more detail on how to do this later.

HAIR TYPES

This information gives a deeper understanding of hair types you can encounter as a stylist.

Below is a special table showing the codes for the 12 different hair types. The scale starts with straighter hair types, right through to extremely tight kinky hair and all other variations in-between.

STRAIGHT HAIR has a round shape:
1a: very straight, fine, shiny, easily becomes oily
1b: straight with thicker volume at the roots
1c: super thick and heavy, extremely difficult to hold curl

1a 1b 1c

WAVY HAIR is considered more oval in shape:
2a: inconsistent soft wavy pattern, sits between wavy and straight
2b: more visual S shape curls, with frizzy texture
2c: strongest S shape curl, very frizzy and dehydrated

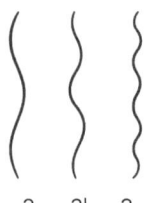
2a 2b 2c

CURLY HAIR is oval in shape (ellipse shape):
3a: defined by full healthy spiral curls, with wider circumference
3b: spiral curls with a smaller curl pattern
3c: thinner hair with smallest diameter spiral curl

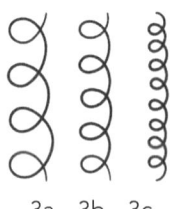
3a 3b 3c

KINKY HAIR has a flatter oval shape:
4a: springy and loosely packed S coils, prone to natural breakage and dryness
4b: densely packed zigzag shaped coil, fluffy like cotton candy
4c: very thick Afro-like coils, excessive dryness, incredible natural volume

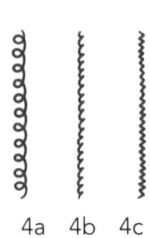
4a 4b 4c

HAIR ELASTICITY

Did you know some hair can stretch up to 20% of its own length when dry, and 65% when wet?

Good hair elasticity is the ability to stretch the hair without losing its natural shape. It's also an indicator of the hair having good moisture and being in a healthy state. If the elasticity is poor, it will be the opposite.

When perming for example, an elasticity test helps you to select the correct rod size to give the desired curl results. If the test indicates the elasticity as poor, then it would be necessary to select a smaller size diameter rod, to ensure the curl result is achieved.

Today the same concept applies for the selection of thermal tools, hot rollers, and even the correct selection of round brushes for blow-drying. If the hair has great elasticity, and you want a loose lazy curl, you can confidently select a larger diameter hot tool and get great results.

Unfortunately, this rule will not apply to hair with weak elasticity, and you will need to drop down one or two diameter sizes in your choice of hot tool to get the same loose lazy curl result.

To give a more practical example of elasticity, take two elastic bands – one rubber and the other nylon. Now stretch both and observe the results. The rubber band will immediately spring back to its original shape. The nylon band does not spring back, and instead remains stretched out and larger than its original size. In summary, the rubber band has good elasticity, while the nylon band has poor elasticity.

The elasticity test is nothing new, and stylists have been doing this test for years. It's very simple to do and will avoid disappointment when a long-lasting curl result is desired.

Performing the Elasticity test:

This test checks the condition of the cortex and the hair strength. As I've covered, when you stretch a rubber elastic band, it will spring back to its original form. And remember, wet hair is more elastic than when it's dry.

The best way to do the test is on slightly damp hair. Select a single hair, pinching it at the roots, then with your thumb and first fingers, run your fingers along the hair stretching the strand to the ends and hold to the count of 10. I'd recommend testing three stands, choosing each from different areas of the head to get a more consistent test result.

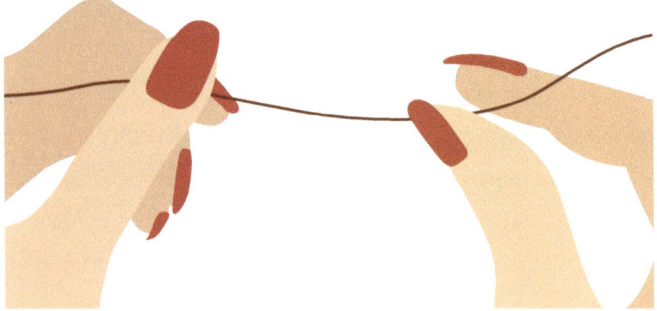

If the hair strands spring and coil back to their original shape, then it has good elasticity.

If it stays stretched out and goes limp or straight, then the elasticity is very poor. This hair type is prone to breakage.

Since I began doing this quick test prior to using thermal tools, blow-drying or hair setting, the results have been amazing – long-lasting springy curls and bouncy blow-dries! This quick test removes the guesswork, giving you confidence to achieve your goals.

HAIR POROSITY

Porosity is the ability of the hair to absorb and hold moisture. Porosity affects how the hair reacts with products, styling techniques or tools. It is measured in three categories: low, medium, and high porosity.

A simple way to test porosity is to take a section of hair between your two fingers and push the hair towards the roots, just like 'backcombing' the hair. If it stays tangled, it's overly porous, if however, it lies down smooth, then it's deemed to have ideal porosity.

Low Porosity is due to a tightly closed hair cuticle – this type of hair has difficulty absorbing moisture and is shiny and silky in appearance. It's often referred to as 'glassy' hair. When confronted with this hair type, I would not recommend using conditioner prior to styling, so the cuticle will not close down and has the ability to absorb styling products. The aim is to give a slightly rough texture, making the hair easier to work with. Using a combination of medium hold mousse and thermal styling spray when preparing the hair will help create a great texture for this hair type.

The hair has difficulty obtaining moisture, but once the moisture is absorbed it will remain moisturised.

Medium Porosity hair absorbs and retains moisture well. The cuticle is generally healthy and normal. This hair type is a pleasure to work with, but will still need a thermal styling spray when preparing, to give it malleable texture. To maintain the quality and integrity of the hair, avoid excessive heat and always adjust hot tools to suit the hair type. This hair type always has the tendency to hold the style well provided the above recommendations are followed.

The hair cuticles are loose, allowing moisture to be easily absorbed and retained.

High Porosity hair absorbs moisture quickly, but doesn't have the ability to retain the moisture. The cuticle is damaged and remains open in areas, mainly due to chemical damage, overuse of hot tools, and the environment. Due to the nature and damage of this type of hair, using a repair serum or porosity equaliser applied to the most damaged parts of the hair will give an even canvas to better prepare for the styling process. Do not use styling tools on high heat to avoid dehydration and additional damage.

The hair easily absorbs moisture, but also easily loses moisture.

The images show the various types of porosity and how the cuticle is affected from low to highly porous hair.

Please note that it's also important to consider the cuticle when looking at hair porosity. The hair cuticle is the outside part of the hair shaft - it helps me to imagine it like the scales on a fish. Formed from dead cells that appear as overlapping protective layers, they help strengthen the hair shaft.

These cuticle scales are made up of a protein called keratin and are easily damaged with heated tools, excessive colouring, and the harsh environment. When the hair has been damaged, the scales break off and leave gaps, making the hair extremely porous.

A simple way to understand highly porous hair is comparing it to a wall needing a paint job. Think about the wall this way - it's cracked, flaking in parts, damp, and faded. These characteristics are similar to high porosity hair. Prior to painting the wall, it needs a lot of preparation to deliver a smooth professional finish. The same principle applies to hair preparation.

HAIR DENSITY

Hair density is based on how much hair is growing on the scalp per square centimetre, or how tightly packed the hairs are growing together. The higher the density, the better the hair will hold volume, curl, and structure.

It's important not to confuse this with hair thickness. Hair thickness is the size each individual hair measures. Note that all hair thickness types can range from low to high density.

Low Density is referred to as having fewer hairs growing per square centimetre, giving the ability to see the scalp easily. Generally, you'll need to use techniques to add volume, which we've covered elsewhere. Consider the addition of hairpieces, and choose products designed to help hold the style.

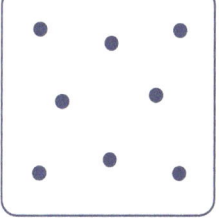

High density

Medium Density means the hairs are growing closer together and covering the scalp more. This type of hair density tends to hold styles quite well.

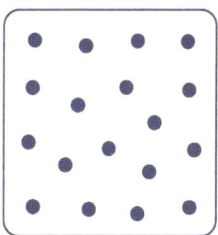

Medium density

High Density is where the hair grows very tightly packed together, making it difficult to part the hair. You can still have very fine individual hairs, but have extremely dense hair. You may need additional help in controlling the hair, such as using appropriate products and techniques that I cover throughout this book.

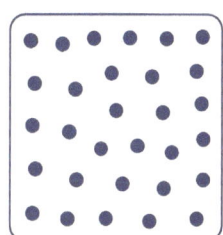

Low density

The images demonstrate the number of hairs per square centimetre and the different levels of density.

HAIR LENGTH

The length of the hair will affect the design decision and the ability to achieve the desired style. Additional techniques, tools, or hairpieces may be required to assist in achieving the results. There seems to be a misconception that hair needs to be super long to achieve an up-style. At times excess length can inadvertently create problems for you.

In fact, different lengths of the hair can be a major issue when determining what hairstyle would work best. For example, when confronted with extra-long hair that sits well below the bra strap at the back, it can send any stylist into a tailspin! When creating an up-do, the challenge is how to compact the excess length into a small enough look to fit the surface size of the scalp, and how to secure it correctly to hold.

I have a great solution to compact excessive length or bulk when doing an up-do.

Firstly, determine how much hair is needed for the design and clip this out of your way. Then scalp braid the remaining hair – this could be in the form of a horizontal braid across the nape if planning a lower design at the nape, or if creating a French roll, consider an internal wide vertical braid up the centre back. These options will help remove excess bulk while allowing a great foundational base to pin the hair into place securely.

Working with layered shorter length hair can present the opposite challenge of not having enough hair to work with, but with the vast array of wefts and extensions on offer, we're spoiled for choice. My recommendation is to explore the best options and work them into the finished design. With so many tools, different types of hairpieces, wigs, hair topper pieces, and styling products currently available, even the shortest head of hair can look luscious in an up-do.

I also recommend asking for a recent photo of the client or models' hair length taken from all angles to allow time to plan a suitable style for the upcoming event or shoot. It will take stress away and allow a plan for success.

I'm a firm believer that with all the styling products and hairpieces available, mixed with lots of imagination and practice, you'll be able to confront any styling challenge that comes your way. The key is preparation and knowing the length and type of hair you're working with before determining the design or modifications required to achieve the style.

There is no limit to what can be achieved, the only limit is our imagination!

CHAPTER 4

STYLING TOOLS AUDIT

*'Develop a passion for learning.
If you do, you will never cease to grow.'*

— ANTHONY J. D'ANGELO

Leading hairdressers will attest to the importance of always using the best equipment and high-quality hair styling products.

Even if it means having to take your time to make that special purchase – because the difference between a low and top-quality tool is like investing in a Ferrari…. more often than not, you get what you pay for.

It's about performance, look and feel, the ergonomics, the technology utilised, whether premium quality materials have been used, and the research and development that goes into developing a new tool so that it delivers on its promise. What you actually achieve with the tool is then up to your skill set.

The market is saturated with hairdressing equipment and it's a minefield sorting out the good from the bad. Do your research before getting caught up with the latest *'it'* tool that social media influencers are promoting…. remember that it's possible they've been paid thousands of dollars to endorse a new tool.

Always check out reviews, ask industry colleagues for their thoughts, watch demonstrations, and pay attention to what professional hair experts are saying before making your decision. And when possible, try before you buy.

Like most things in life, products and equipment never stop evolving. Just because it's new, doesn't always mean it's better. Just because it's top dollar doesn't always mean it's the best. You need to weigh up the pros and cons and decide what's best for you and your needs, and make an informed decision.

The following pages are jam-packed with lots of product information – from combs to hair nets, you'll start to become an authority on what's best for the job!

COMBS

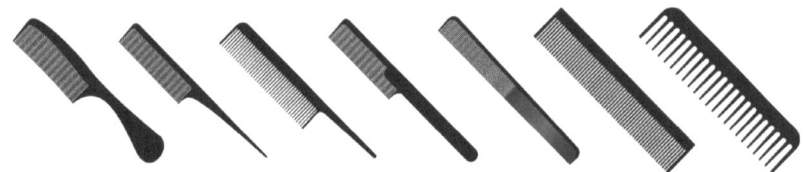

Carbon fibre combs are the most commonly used today. They're static free and have more rounded teeth which are gentler on the scalp. The most important feature is that they won't melt when blow-drying or used near hot tools.

**Please absolutely throw away your old combs when the teeth have snags, or are bent or broken. They're impossible to work with and you'll never achieve beautiful styling with inferior tools.

One of the most popular comb brands on the market today is the YS *Park* range. Created by Mr Young Soo Park, the range is huge with combs designed for all different hair services. The braid comb for example, has a shorter length tail that sits comfortably in the palm of your hand, with shorter width and narrower spaced teeth, and it gives a clean defined finish to any scalp braid.

I teach the following information in all my hair styling classes – it's my theory on what comb to use when, because it's not a matter of one comb suits all situations.

With different combs you can expect different results. I also like to think of my fingers as a comb, especially when wanting a deconstructed finish. When raking your fingers through soft curls, you get a softer dishevelled, casual feel to the curls. Don't expect a super polished finish, it's more like using a wind machine or throwing the head down and back to get lots of airy texture.

The next stage of dressing hair is replacing your fingers with an extra wide tooth comb. The preferable option is an extra-wide static-free comb. You'll achieve a more polished, controlled finish to the look. Use this to relax curls and comb those popular Hollywood waves in place.

The wider teeth will show line marks when you comb through the hair, giving a more modern and 'lived in' vibe.

A narrow tooth comb will give the ultimate smooth polished finish to the hair. If you want to achieve a mirror glass finish to a classic chignon for example, always use the finest or narrowest spaced teeth available.

I like to use a metal end tail comb when setting and tonging to help smooth and sleek the surface of a tight clean ponytail. Make sure you run your fingers along the metal tail surface to check it is free of chips or small catches that could snag the hair. Don't let this problem become your worst nightmare!

To sum up combs, I always like to first plan my finished styles and what I aim to achieve. Then I select the best comb that will deliver the best possible results – it's all about what you imagine the finished style to be and what you want to achieve. Select the right comb to get the job done – fingers or wider teeth for looser casual looks, and a finer tooth comb for sleek polished finishes.

HAIRBRUSHES

When it comes to hairbrushes, we're spoiled for choice! So, it's best to understand the difference between brushes, and when to use which one.

Dressing-out brush (teasing brush)

Designed for teasing and dressing hair, this little gem packs a punch. They've been in the marketplace for years, and every seasoned stylist would have one in their kit.

It gives a light fluffy texture when used for teasing the hair, but isn't suitable when a strong solid teased foundation is required. This narrow-base nylon bristle brush is densely spaced with 4 rows of firm bristles. Some offer a variety of bristle lengths within the brush. The handle is generally pointed, and this is somewhat helpful with sectioning the hair.

This brush was very popular in the 1960s when big bouffant styles were worn – they were used to tease internally, then to smooth over the outer surface of the hair to form the design. Please note that this brush is not recommended for blow-drying.

Suitable for:
- Sleeking the hair into a ponytail
- Ideal for dressing-out both long and shorter lengths
- Teasing the hair into a puffy ball shape, covering with a fine hair net, and using this as an internal hair padding shape

Cushion base brush

There are various companies who sell cushion-based styling brushes. The unique feature of the cushion base brush is the domed rubber shape cushion where the bristles are planted into the cushion. The cushion is designed to fill with air when brushing the scalp, giving a more luxurious and comfortable experience.

The most famous cushion brush is manufactured by *Mason Pearson* and was created 130 years ago! This range of brushes continue to be the 'brush of choice' used by leading session stylists due to their ability to deliver a shiny polished finish to the hair. This iconic range of brushes still outperforms competitors – even with the hefty price tag, it's still the most coveted.

The bristles are made from boar bristles, with a choice of different lengths that suit different hair lengths and thickness. Whether it's an original *Mason Pearson* brush or a copy of one, you have a choice of either 100% boar, or a brush with a mix of boar/nylon bristles.

Suitable for:
- Brushing thick, long hair
- Styling and dressing various length hair
- Occasionally used for directionally blow-drying, smoothing, and sleeking a clean ponytail

Mixed bristle brush

With a combination of boar and nylon bristles, this brush is also known as a 'porcupine' due to its 'tufted bristles'.

Suitable for:
- Coarse hair as it penetrates through the thick hair deep into the scalp

Vent brush

Normally made from plastic with small balls on the end of the tips to protect the scalp. The vent brush has wide spaces that allow the air to flow through the hair, enabling the hair to dry faster.

The newer style vent brushes are a similar design to a large padding brush, but with wider spaced bristles.

Suitable for:
- Excellent for shorter hair styling where natural movement is desired
- Not designed for blow-drying curls as the spaces lack control and tension

Wet Brush

One of the latest brushes to hit the market, the wet brush is designed to detangle wet long hair, avoiding pulling and breakage. The slightly curve-shaped base contours the head for comfort, and the open vented plastic bristles speed up drying.

Suitable for:
- Brushing out beach or loose 'Instagram-style curls'
- Detangling natural and kinky hair prior to drying

Round ceramic brush

This brush comes in a variety of different diameters. The smaller the diameter, the tighter the curl. I recommend using a barrel made with a vented aluminium core and a shorter length bristle. The metal core heats up from the blow-dryer, allowing the hair to dry faster and giving a stronger curl. A round brush will produce defined movement, flicks, and various curl sizes. Note that due to the nature of this brush, it can over-dry and dehydrate the hair.

Suitable for:
- All hair types
- Perfect for traditional on base blow-drying

Paddle brush

A paddle brush has a wide cushioned base with widely spaced bristles. This brush will pull easily through the hair, without stretching the hair. Perfect for directional blow-drying and helping control static, allowing for a better air flow.

Suitable for:
- Straight, long hair blow-drying
- Directional root drying
- General long hair brushing

Denman brush

Made with a rubber base planted with nylon bristles, the Denman is available in 7 or 9 rows of bristles. The more rows, the deeper the 'C' curve of the brush. The flexible rubber base smooths the cuticle and promotes shine. Not recommended to achieve a curly result.

Suitable for:
- Blow-drying classic precision haircuts when a bevelled finish is desired
- Brushing fine to thick hair
- Directional and wrap drying from shorter to longer lengths

ELASTICS AND HAIR TIES

There are so many different types of elastics, band types, and hair ties available to suit whatever task you wish to achieve. I've got my favourites, but with so many options available, I do like to test drive anything new to make sure I'm using the best, and recommending the best to my students.

Let's take a look at what I like to use, plus a few additional options for you to consider.

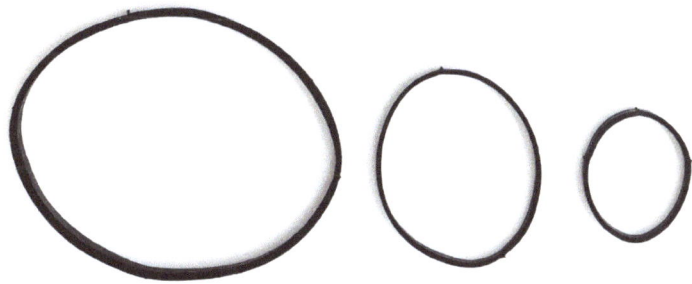

Hat elastic

This elastic is great to secure a clean polished runway pony. Some stylists use a piece of elastic as an alternative to using elastic bands – add a knot on each end, then add bobby pins through the knots to secure. Available by the metre from a craft or haberdashery store, my preferred size is 2mm or 3mm in diameter.

Rubber bands

I prefer to use these types of bands with my up-styling as I can adjust the tension when I wrap around a base, especially when securing a ponytail. Size 14 is a perfect size for all thickness of hair. Generally purchased in bulk from a stationery or office supply store.

Small elastic hair bands

These are great when you need a tiny band to finish off a braid or twist. Using small elastic bands gives you the option to pull open a braid and avoid the hair catching or snagging in the braid. Available from equestrian stores, these bands are generally used for braiding horse manes and/or tails. They're very strong and available in 6 different colours, which makes it easy to colour match most hair colours.

Anti-snag nylon bands

This type of band is the most commonly used band, but it's my least preferred band to use, due to its inability to stretch well and spring back. It limits the ability to pull open or distress braids and twists without snagging and over texturing the hair, leaving the finished look messy and unfinished. However, it can be a good option when used at the end of a braid to finish off.

Bungee hair ties

These are a single piece of elastic covered with cotton with metal hooks attached to both ends. They are widely used today but I'm not a fan. I personally don't like the way the hair tends to split and gape open where the hooks are attached. Where they shine is for daily use to protect the hair from band damage.

Bungee hair tape

This is the latest technology that secures your style without bands. It bonds to itself by simply wrapping around the base of a pony or braid. I don't feel it's strong enough to hold the hair together to form a secure base, rather it's more to decorate and finish off the look.

Eco hair ties

These bands are super strong, and don't slip or loosen up. They come in various sizes, and as the name suggests, they are environmentally friendly and created from recycled bike tyre tubes. You can't get a better option if sustainability is important to you.

Spiral rings

This spiral-shaped plastic ring is a very interesting way to hold the hair together with an extra strong grip. It doesn't tangle in wet or dry hair. I don't like to use them when styling hair as I can't achieve a clean finish with the hair. They are more of a fun and reliable tie for those who want that lived-in hair look.

Cotton bound elastic bands

These bands are a must have for everyday hair styling, especially for young ones with long hair. They don't tangle as much and are easier to remove. They don't have the ability to stretch and retract back like a regular band does. Hence, they can't give the firmer strong hold necessary when creating long hairstyles.

PINS

Let's explore what pins are available, working through what's hot and not so hot! It's super important to get to know in-depth what's best and why.

Bobby pins

Bobby pins are made of a long narrow piece of flat metal, folded in half, and pressed back against itself, allowing the hair to be held between the two sides with pressure. You'll find some bobby pins have a ripple and others will be smooth and flat in shape.

There is so much conversation around the best bobby pin to use! From Japanese to Chinese to French manufactured pins, from ripples versus no ripples.

To be perfectly honest it's all about personal choice, and what you're comfortable using. I definitely prefer to use the ripple bobby pins, not the smooth non-ripple variety.

Bobby pins generally come in three different lengths. The shorter length is recommended to be used in finer hair. Medium length is the standard size bobby pin most commonly used by stylists when dressing hair, and the longer length pin is recommended to hold extra thick, heavy weighted long hair.

The shorter length bobby pin is great for holding more textured styles. It's always hard to hide longer pins when working with these textures, and placing an unopened short pin, woven into the base of the design, will hold really well.

The medium length bobby pin is my go-to. I use them in 90% of my designs. I always like to have a variety of different colours to match different hair colours.

Fringe pins

A standard fringe pin is not pressurised, but instead open in a 'U' shape. My personal preference when dressing hair is the ripple pin option, not the smooth flat non ripple pin. I feel the ripple gives a better grip, making it easier to open, and overall, stronger in its design.

I never recommend using the fringe pin to hold hair in place, they are just not strong. Over the years I have figured out what I like to use and have developed a lot of tricks to make them work perfectly for me.

Invisible hair pins

This is a very fine wire u-pin, typically used for up-dos. They are great when that random flyaway needs to be controlled. Or when you need to secure a section of hair where a regular bobby pin would be difficult to hide. Some stylists bend the tip of the u-pin back on itself to help lock into the hair better. I don't advise using these to secure a typical up-do as they are not strong enough to hold securely.

HAIR CLIPS

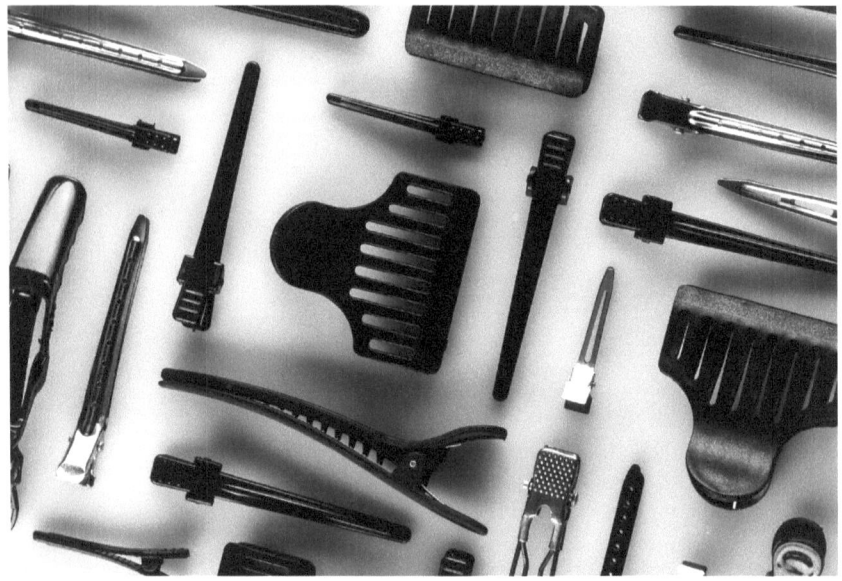

These are known to be the very first styling invention, with a long rich history. There are some fantastic sectioning clips on the market today that are designed to be used in a variety of ways. The clips I'm about to talk about are known as 'tools of the trade', while the other plentiful options you'll find out there are trendy decorative hair clips. Made from plastic, aluminium, and strong metal, they come in all shapes and sizes designed for many different purposes.

Alligator clips

The plastic alligator clip is perfect for holding hair in place, and they are particularly good for holding long heavy hair while blow-drying or holding hair while cutting. The internal teeth are quite aggressive, hence their name! They are made from heavy plastic that is lightweight and durable.

Serrated clips

Generally used when doing a very technical haircut, I prefer the long slender metal clip with internal serrated teeth. They have extra strong springs to prevent even very fine hair from slipping, and they grab the hair well, whilst being strong but not bulky to use. Never use these clips when styling hair.

Long duck bill clips

Even the slightest serration inside a clip will catch and snag the hair. When styling hair, this clip is my preferred clip, as it doesn't have serrations. The gentle curve sits comfortably on the scalp, and they have a smooth strong metal finish both inside and out. Perfect when holding heavy hair and using it to secure sections while styling any long hair design.

Paddle clips

This metal single prong clip has a plastic paddle attached to one side of the clip. It's a multipurpose clip designed for holding the hair flat, or around the face or fringe without leaving any demarcation lines or marks. Hint: be careful when removing the clip to avoid the edge of the plastic paddle catching in the hair.

Single prong clips

This clip comes in either plastic or metal material, and in either single or double prongs. My preference is a metal clip with a single prong. There are many different options available - lightweight longer pointed clips (difficult to find) are best suited for styling delicate artistic looks. The strong shorter length clips are best suited for wet pin curl sets.

'Plan each day to try something new.'

– SHARON BLAIN

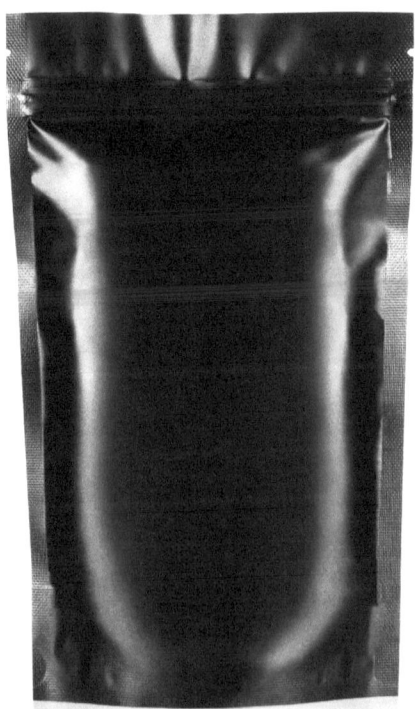

CHAPTER 5

STYLING
PRODUCTS

The different range of styling products available on the market today is enormous. The major challenge is to sift through all the options available to find what works best for you.

Most stylists have a favourite brand and will be happy to give you their views on what's great and not so great about the various ranges.

Like them, I've got my favourite styling products that I've used forever, but I also enjoy testing new products to ensure I've got the best option that enhances my work. It's important to test new products and keep an open mind as different options come through.

Following is a list of the key types of styling products available:

Hair serum: A thick liquid-based treatment with a silicone base, this is used to coat the surface of the hair. It gives overall protection to the hair and helps to smooth frizz, while adding shine. Ideal for thick unruly curls, and great for very dry hair. Use sparingly to avoid weighing down fine to medium hair, or relaxing voluminous curls.

Curl defining creme: This is a leave-in conditioning product used to give well defined curls on curly to kinky hair types. It will fight frizz, can be applied to damp or dry hair, and some have heat activated technology to keep the curls naturally bouncy. Not to be confused with hair serum that's silicone based, defining creme is a thicker consistency and will weigh the hair down. It contains shea butter, coconut oils, and other plant-based extracts.

Mousse: Has a foam consistency and I recommend it's applied to damp hair. Designed to prepare the hair prior to blow-drying and wet setting. Available in medium to strong hold, it will add root volume, control frizz, and give strong bouncy curls. Look out for some mousses that have a higher alcohol content – this makes the hair tacky and grippy to work with.

Thermal styling spray: Thermal styling sprays work in a few different ways – they normally have a hold factor of 3-4, acting as a protective barrier over the hair cuticle aiding in protecting the hair from intense

heat from hot tools and blow-drying. Thermal sprays help to reduce moisture loss and protect against hair dehydration. Due to the hold factor, the additional bonus is that it delivers volume and bounce, a luxe smooth finish, and cuts the drying time in most products in half.

Hair gel: Has a jelly like consistency and is available in light through to stronger hold. It will dry, harden, and dehydrate the hair. Hair gel is ideal when used to control frizz, kinky hair texture, or to deliver a 'wet look' finish. Combining strong gel and moisturising cream together will allow the hair to be pliabile when styling or moulding shapes. *'Gorilla Snot'* is known as one the strongest available.

Sea salt spray: A wet styling product containing paraben-free sea salt and sea kelp that adds volume and texture for a beach wave look. Its lightweight consistency is suitable for all hair types, especially finer hair. Used on wet or dry hair, it adds a rough feel to the hair shaft, giving fullness and the ability to separate curls for a modern dishevelled look.

Heat protection spray: A leave-in product that protects the hair from heat damage when using hot tools and blow-drying. Available in either a spray, cream, or serum, it helps seal in moisture and maintain hydration. It adds shine and polish to the finished look but doesn't have any hold factor. Think of heat protection as sunscreen for your hair!

Texture powder: A dust like product offering an extremely lightweight texture made from silica silylate, or rice powder. The powder like fibres coat the hair, adding a matt finish that gives thickness and a gripping texture. It's important to test different options, making sure that the powder is super fine – avoid powder with noticeable particles.

Spray wax: A flexible spray in wax form. Comes as an aerosol and will hold the hair in place, giving a wax-like shine with bendable smooth strands. Unlike hair spray that only holds, spray wax will hold, but also allows the ability to create more specific detailed effects with the hair such as small separated and soft textures. Will help maintain an airy, light, voluminous feel without looking over-sprayed and plastic.

Shine spray: A weightless ultra-fine mist that adds shine and controls unruly textures and fluff. Shine spray must dry extra fast to avoid developing an oily slick and weighing down the hair. Used in conjunction with a medium hold hair spray, it helps add a polished hold during the styling process.

Hair spray: Available in either pump or aerosol, it comes in a light working spray, medium hold, or super strong and lacquers. A quick drying spray, it's often used to hold the hair in place and protect it from wind and humidity. Working spray is recommended to use during the styling process as it is very light, and not as sticky or tacky on the hair.

MY FAVOURITE PRODUCTS

The products I've just listed are my suggestions to add to your styling kit. Always have one of each on hand to cover all hair types and any styling challenge that comes your way.

Out of necessity, I have managed to reduce the number of products I use on a day-to-day basis down to the bare minimum. Between a weightless shine spray, thermal styling spray, medium hold hair spray, and spray wax, I can cover 95% of the looks I do.

Plus, I also like to use a heat protector spray for blow-drying, hot roller, thermal sets, wet finger waves and pin-curl setting. And lastly, I never leave home without a variety of serums, cuticle and moisture sealants.

Remember that the right product will always deliver exceptional results, but the wrong choice or misuse of a product can create a styling nightmare! Being prepared is an essential part of styling, and yet it's a step that is often overlooked or downplayed.

Preparation for different hair types

Correctly analysing the hair prior to styling in order to make the best product selection will go a long way in helping you deliver a beautiful finish.

I always pay particular attention to the porosity of the hair, the hair texture, and if I'm thermal setting, then I also check the hair elasticity.

If you need to balance uneven or poor porosity throughout the hair, I suggest you add a *porosity equaliser* on damp hair, which will also seal the cuticle and replace lost moisture. A porosity equaliser is a leave-in protein treatment that strengthens the hair internally, targeting damaged hair and equalising poor porosity. Consider adding a cuticle sealer to unruly curls and frizzy hair types prior to preparing for styling.

HANDLING FINE HAIR

One of the biggest hair challenges I find is when styling long fine silky soft hair. The stress of creating long lasting curls used to send me into a panic! This hair type is also very slippery to tease, lacking texture and root volume. Even to get a pin to hold in this hair type can be difficult.

After years of trial and error, I'm confident to recommend this hair hack favourite, and hopefully it will help keep your stress levels under control when styling fine hair.

The key when working with fine hair, and even any other type of hair, is to add grip and build texture. The hair texture should feel like a coarse cotton fabric.

To begin with, I suggest adding a medium hold mousse to damp hair, rough drying it into the hair. From here, if the hair still feels soft, repeat a second mousse application, and at the same time dampen the hair with a thermal spray. Then blow-dry with a brush to give a polished finish.

At this stage the soft hair texture should now feel coarser and rougher to touch.

On a side note, use a mousse without a high level of alcohol to avoid a sticky feel or too much dry crunch in the hair, as it will make styling hair very difficult.

This is where I'm often asked, "will adding salt spray or texture powder help?". Yes, they can, but it's not necessary. Both will give lots of grip, but on very fine hair they can make the hair very difficult to style. The hair will look matt dry with an unruly difficult texture, and can lack polish when finished.

You need to test your products beforehand so styling on that special day will be a pleasure rather than a styling disaster for both you and the client.

CHAPTER 6

BRAIDS

'The only place where success comes before work is in the dictionary.'

– VIDAL SASSOON

If you look at the history of hair braiding, it dates back at least 5,000 years! And African hair braiding can even be traced back to 2500 B.C.E.

Although many cultures claim sole credit for the braid, it's difficult to trace it back to any one single origin. From Asia, Egypt, the Americas, African tribes, and even Europe, they all have a history of braiding mainly worn as a convenient solution to keep hair tidy, or for celebrations and social events.

A braid is also known as a plait, and is created when two or more strands of hair are interlaced in a repetitive woven pattern. The most traditional braid is a flat three strand woven structure. Different tribes decorated their braids with the likes of feathers, string, wool, and leather.

Throughout my years in the industry, I've seen braiding trends come and go. I can recall in the sixties a trend when small braids were wound through big, looped curls in a bouffant for added effect. Or thick braids were wired to stand in loops on top of the head.

Having such a fascination for braids, I booked a ticket to London in the early 1970s to study at Molten Browns. They were seen as the braid masters of the time, and were teaching very creative ways of braiding – I still use these techniques today.

Around the same period some of my favourite hair idols; Trevor Sorbie, Anthony Mascola, and Robert Lobetta, were also experimenting with different woven and braiding techniques, and the latest hair magazines were full of their work. These iconic images can still be seen today, showcasing intricate polished basket woven heads, rope twists, and pinched hair veils done with such precision and many hours of work. These guys set the trends and continued to do so for many years.

A special moment in my hair journey takes me back some 30-plus years in New York City. The salon *Gandini from Italy* had me spellbound when they presented a stunning show at a NYC beauty show. I'd never seen such an incredible show with such beautiful braiding. I recall videoing these techniques and sitting for weeks practicing and perfecting them. They intrigued me with the way they incorporated ribbons into these unique braiding techniques, with some looks sitting high off the head, and others woven down the back at various angles.

Another beautiful memory was watching Alexandre' De Paris work his magic – he is in my opinion, the greatest long hair master of our time. I still remember the exquisite braid he created on stage. Using extra-long fine hair nets, he covered different sections with the nets, and wove the sections into a waist length intricate braid, adorning it with stunning jewellery. It wasn't that it was such a complicated look to achieve that made it so memorable, but rather the simplicity of the overall look. The greatest lesson I learned that day is 'simplicity is *the* key to dressing long hair', and how a simple braid executed to perfection can demand a standing ovation.

In the late 1980s and 1990s, hippy and grunge was all the rage. Pigtails with different braids, or curls with tiny side braids, was the hottest fun trend, especially for parties, concerts and festivals.

I also remember my own first how-to books and videos where I taught many different braid techniques and how to include braids as part of an up-do. This material was developed nearly twenty years ago now, but I look back with pride when I see the finished looks. Who would believe the looks I did back then still continue to be in demand today!

Granted my braiding videos don't have the rough finish textures of the current trends, but that's to be expected as looks and techniques evolve. I'm often asked how long I think this braiding trend will last. Or will braiding techniques just continue to evolve? I'm not sure if we've exhausted all the options of where the humble braid can go next. But who knows…let's watch this space!

At the time of writing this book, the resurgence of braiding is at an all-time high, and the variation of different types of braids on offer today is just incredible. You can't open social media or YouTube without a quick tutorial popping up, and you can spend hours learning the latest 'It' braids from the next generation of famous stylists all over Instagram.

Here's what you need to know about braiding – you need to have nimble fingers, lots of patience, and heaps of time to perfect them. For some, braiding comes naturally, but for others it just doesn't click, and it's such a challenge.

I love the way so many younger stylists are constantly creating different types of braids, challenging themselves to create something new, and experimenting by incorporating different colour hairpieces, adding soft textures, fab clips, or weaving chains into a braid to offer a different twist on a popular classic. These braiding influencers are changing the way we think about braids for generations to come.

The list of different types of braids is extensive – from the waterfall, fishtail, three strand inside and outside braid, knot braid, band braid, infinity braid, four strand, basket weave, scalp braid, and rope braids and twists to name a few.

When I'm often asked, 'what braids should I learn to add to my skill set, and to help me meet the current trends?', I will always recommend learning a scalp braid, the three strand inside and outside braid, and a rope and single twist braid. The rest are great to know, but only if you want to offer a more specialised braid service.

Here's why I always recommend these particular options:

SCALP BRAID

This one is important to know if you plan to sew wefts into the hair, to add thickness and bulk to lower density hair.

Generally, one or two scalp braids are placed horizontally around the head, beginning back from the hairline. You may need to add extra rows if more bulk is needed. I recommend using a curved needle and linen thread to attach the wefts. It's important to make sure you use good tension and make sure it's clean and precise.

Depending on the weight of the weft being attached, you must ensure

the width of the braid is wide enough to avoid pulling the hair. A general rule of thumb is 1 cm wide.

The scalp braid is also fantastic for attaching bridal veils, hair accessories, or even hats into the hair without the need for bobby pins. Select the spot on the head where the veil is to be placed. Section off horizontally a 1cm wide section, or about the width of the comb being used, add a clean scalp braid across the head, and finish off with a small elastic band. I'd recommend doing the braid first, and setting or styling after. Use your fingers to feel the braid below, and when ready, slip the teeth of the comb into the braid, and you're ready to go.

Apart from creating fabulous contemporary or avant-garde looks using scalp braids, they are also great when attaching a wire cage, padding, or avant-garde hairpieces onto the head. Scalp braids create the base to attach these, and they are strong enough to sew into, and will hold wire shape in place with ease.

SINGLE TWISTS

I don't believe there are many styles today that don't include either a rope braid or twist. To achieve beautiful textured up-do's, take sections around the head and do a few twists around the crown, then gently pull out the edges of the twist to create volume and soft texture with an airy romantic feel to the hair.

    I certainly recommend spraying a light weightless shine spray onto the twist to avoid creating a fuzzy messy texture when pulling the pieces out from the twist. A lot of the hairstyles in the latest runway shows have been very clean ballet buns, and the single twist has been used to achieve these buns. They are covered with a fine hair net and pinned tightly at the nape. I love how chic and polished they look, and the bun is always timeless and so beautiful.

ROPE TWIST

This technique is perfect when you want a clean top knot bun or a beautiful, twisted chignon on the nape. One of my favourite ways to achieve the twisted nape chignon is to place a chopstick horizontally in behind the back of the nape ponytail. Use either a rope twist or single twist with the ponytail and loop the tail across the chopstick in a figure eight, and then gently pull it out.

The rope twist has the ability to pull out easily, provided the twist is not over twisted. When you over twist the hair, the hair locks itself together, so be mindful that you practice to what degree you need to twist for the perfect result. This braid is often used as a centrepiece to weave individual sections of hair throughout to create a mermaid look.

INSIDE AND OUTSIDE BRAIDS

When looking at current wedding hair on Pinterest, at least 65% has some sort of braid incorporated into the looks. Be it a pony with a braid at the front, a nape chignon with braids at the side, or a half up-half down look with a circle braid.

Some of the braids are created with the inside technique, while the others with an outside braid. Most of these braids have been textured and expanded and opened wide. I personally like the way the outside braid opens out, as it gives a beautiful shell effect along the braid. The outside pick-up braid shows more definition and looks great when pulled out as a circular braid.

BRAIDING HAIR HACKS

- Always use clean sections and parting when braiding

- Keep good tension throughout the braiding process

- Medium hold gel can be used to control layers and help keep good tension when creating scalp braids

- Lightly spray the hair with weightless shine spray to control unnecessary frizz when opening out the braids

- For clean scalp braids, spray thermal spray on the hair to help create tight clean braids

- Use a braid comb when creating clean tight scalp braids

- Never use hair spray or texture powder when pulling out the braids as it will create frizz and messy texture

- When braiding fine hair, use a tool like my ELEVATE PRO STYLER volumiser at the roots to pump up the volume and make the braids look thicker

- Use long fringe pins when creating the design to hold the open braids in place

- A light spray wax can be use in moderation to help set the open braids in place

I have created an online learning platform if you are keen to get into learning my different braiding techniques and styles that incorporate a variety of braids. You can see more at sharonblain.com

CHAPTER 7

CURL SCIENCE AND THEORY

'In order to be irreplaceable,

one must always be different.'

– COCO CHANEL

I want to take a step back and share the theory behind old-school setting techniques used to create some of the most iconic hair looks we still identify with today.

The common denominator between famous looks like Brigitte Bardot's beehive, Audrey Hepburn's chignon, and Priscilla Presley's bouffant, is that they've all been created with a strong foundational set, or tong setting, to achieve each look.

These old-school techniques are still used today, especially when setting wigs and hairpieces for movies and theatre. It's an important skill to learn and valuable to know if your career path leans towards this area.

Wet setting was the most common way to create curls prior to the mid-1970s.

When I started my apprenticeship, setting was the most important skill to master. Learning different setting patterns, placement of rollers, on or off-base, roller choice, tension, the best products to use, etc all took hours of practice to perfect.

The most booked stylists were the ones who could master a set that could last a week. Setting kept salons extremely busy in those days, and weekly bookings were the norm.

Back then salons always had rows of floor hair dryers installed. It was a juggling act when a head of hair didn't dry as fast as required, as every appointment was tightly scheduled throughout the day.

To grasp the theory on how setting hair works, it's important to understand the fundamental science to achieve long-lasting curls, waves, and bouncy blow-dries.

The science and success behind setting hair is identical to blow-drying, curls in general, finger waves, pin curling, and using thermal tools.

One of the most vital pieces of information to understand is how the hydrogen bonds in the internal hair structure react when water and/or heat is applied so you can achieve the desired outcome – whether this is straight or curly, and regardless of the method you are using.

A simple way to explain a hydrogen bond is to imagine a chain bracelet, with the chain links locking together. A hydrogen bond represents each chain link. When heat or water is applied, the chains swell open, allowing the chain to break apart and be reformed into a new or different shape. Once the hair is dried and cooled, the chain locks back together, but temporarily in the new shape.

An important point to remember is that the hydrogen bonds need time to reform into their new shape. This will only occur when the hair has been allowed to cool down correctly. For example, when curling, my preference is to clip each curl in place while the hair cools down – generally allow a minimum of ten minutes, more if possible, until the hair is cold. If time is an issue, grab a blow-dryer with a diffuser on the COLD setting to speed up the process.

This is also required when doing any styling from wet to dry – the hair must be 100% dried into its new shape and allowed time to cool. The same rules apply when using thermal tools on dry hair – the hair needs to have time to cool into the new shape for the hydrogen bonds to reform into the desired temporary shape or style.

You must also consider the elasticity of the hair and the role this can play when looking for long lasting curls. When the elasticity is weak and does not have the ability to spring back, selecting a tool with a small diameter will help. Back at trade school when learning to perm, the elasticity test determined what size perm rod you would use. I like to use this analysis when deciding the size of my barrel, rollers, or round brush selection.

The same base theory relates to thermal setting, hot roller, and round brush blow-drying – basically every time volume, curl, or a wave result is required, this information needs to be understood.

The base

The type of curl result is determined by a variety of factors: the length of the hair, diameter of the roller, the roller position and the base size. The base placement determines the height and volume. This theory relates to all types of curling techniques, setting, tonging, hot rollers or blow drying. The diagram shows some of the different base placements.

The base is the section of hair where the roller is placed when setting. In almost all cases, the base should be the same length and width as the roller.

There are six different base positions that will determine the outcome of the finished look:

1. On-base
2. Off-base
3. Half-off base
4. Over-directed
5. Under-directed
6. Indentation

On-base is when maximum volume is desired. The hair is lifted at 90 degrees from the base when setting to give the roots guaranteed maximum volume. The section depth is governed by the diameter of the roller. The width of each section should not overlap the roller, but be slightly shorter than the roller. I mainly use on-base placement for all my setting and round brush blow-drying, including thermal setting for maximum root volume.

Off-base minimises the volume, with a flatter base. The hair is directed at 45 degrees from the base and rolled down. The roller sits at the bottom of the base. The size of the base section is the same as the roller diameter.

Half-off base is where only half the roller sits half on and half off the base, creating a medium amount of volume. Comb the hair at 75 degrees and roll the hair downwards.

Over-directed is where the hair is combed forward at 135 degrees past the base for extreme volume. I personally have a theory about over-direction, especially when working with the area from the forehead to the crown on top of the head.

If you take a close look at the root position, the roots lay at 0 degrees of elevation at the scalp. When the hair is dried and brushed back, instead of giving exceptional volume, the roots tend to split open due to gravity and the flatness caused by lack of elevation. I only advise setting over-direction from the crown area, and downwards to the nape.

Under-directed placement is used for absolutely no root volume, with just movement from mid-lengths to ends. The base section is 1.5 to 5 times the diameter of the roller or tool, and the hair section is wider than the base, which is then set in the lowest part of the base, creating drag and minimal volume.

Indentation is when the hair is combed down flat on the scalp and the ends of the hair are rolled upwards. To achieve a dent or hollow, the size of the base must be at least 1.5 times the diameter of the roller. When setting with indentation, the roots are flat on the scalp when brushed out, while the ends of the hair will curl up and flick out from the head.

The stem

The stem of a pin curl also dictates the direction and movement of the hair. A short stem on a pin curl will give more curl but little movement, whereas a longer stem is designed to give greater movement and flexibility when dressing hair into waves.

The curl

This information is extremely important to know because the correct choice of round brush or roller size/diameter will predict the outcome of the finished look.

For a strong curl result, the hair must wrap a minimum of two times around the base of a roller to form an 'S' movement. If the hair lacks elasticity, choose a smaller diameter base to achieve a more predictable outcome.

A combination of 'S' formations will give a strong bouncy curl and good wave result. If the hair wraps only once around the base of the round brush or roller, a 'C' shape will be formed.

Only use an extra-large diameter base when limited movement is required. A combination of 'C' formations can give volume, but very limited curl – think loose gentle movement with this approach.

Setting and blow-drying patterns

There are a few different types of setting patterns all designed to give a different outcome:

- Herringbone pattern
- Directional setting pattern
- C-section pattern
- Brickwork pattern
- Classic set pattern

The diagrams below clearly show these setting patterns:

Herringbone

With this setting pattern, the rollers are placed diagonally around the head in horizontal sections. Setting begins from the top of the head down to the nape. The roller placement is laid out in alternating opposite directions. The herringbone is great to achieve a traditional glamour wave.

Brickwork

This set follows the same pattern as a brick wall, except each roller is placed on-base and follows the curve of the natural head shape. The advantage of using this pattern is that you avoid any separation and parting opening up when styling the hair. The brickwork pattern gives an overall voluminous, bouncy curl result.

Directional setting

When mapping out a specific hair design, choose the directional setting option for a more predictable result. The set can either be on-base or off-base, depending on the plan of the finished style. It can be rolled in a vertical, diagonal, or horizontal direction to achieve the best results.

Classic

This set allows for a more versatile styling option. Beginning at the front hairline, two parallel partings follow the head shape to the nape, leaving a space the same width of the roller between the partings. You can choose different base placements, determining this by the desired outcome. The side section allows for flexibility, set either backwards or forwards, depending on the design.

C-section

This setting pattern is used when a voluminous classic wave movement around the face is required. It's worked in a curved section at the front hairline, using a pie section and on base placement. The rollers curve around the section towards the face. This approach guarantees a perfect wave every time!

SECTIONING AND PARTING

I can't impress upon you the importance of making sure you always focus on creating clean partings and sections.

Clean parting and sections help delineate the various areas on the head prior to setting or drying. Breaking down the hair into small sections gives a good working plan as to where to start the styling process, whether at the front or the nape. It looks more professional and helps to speed up the service.

This image shows good sectioning with clean precise parting, which is essential when styling hair.

PRO CLASSIC SETTING TIPS

1. Make sure the hair is thoroughly and evenly wet to avoid irregular curl results.

2. Ensure you have the same strong tension when wrapping the hair around every roller.

3. Make sure the hair is completely dry and allow to cool down before brushing out.

4. Flat wrapping the hair smooth and clean around the roller gives a more polished curl.

5. Make sure all the sections are the same width as the size of the diameter of the setting rollers.

6. Always choose the roller size based on the type of curl you desire.

7. Use a metal end tail comb to tuck the ends of the hair cleanly around the roller to avoid 'fish hooks' appearing on the ends of the curls.

8. Never forget *'you get what you set'* – don't miss any preparation steps, know the outcome you want before you start, and choose the right techniques to get the desired result!

CHAPTER 8

BLOW-DRYING

'The whole purpose of education is to turn mirrors into windows.'

– SYDNEY J. HARRIS

As I move onto sharing my thoughts and tips for achieving fabulous bouncy blow-dries, be sure to absorb all I've written in Chapter 7 on curl science and theory – it's vital to first understand the science of hair and the role it plays, how it reacts, and the process required for creating fabulous blow-dries, curls, and waves, which all share a common thread when it comes to achieving amazing results.

Now let's get into blow-drying because a perfectly executed blow-dry can light up your client's face with a confidence that almost nothing else does!

A great example of this is how the value of a professional hairdresser was elevated during the Covid-19 pandemic restrictions. Clients spoke about missing their hairdressers so much – and I really believe we have been underestimating the power we have in our hands.

Delivering exceptional customer service and great hair is what keeps clients returning. Which is why it's incredibly important to be a master in all aspects of the craft, and blow-drying is no exception.

A little side note on a flashback to when the first commercial blow-dryer hit the market. I was a young apprentice, and when the dryer landed in the salon, we honestly had no idea how to use it. At first, we would still set the hair in rollers and stood there holding the dryer over the hair until it dried – back then it all seemed so pointless! Over time we moved on to blasting hair dry, and then added Velcro rollers. We finally graduated to using brushes and blow-drying hair, so the rest is history. It's amazing how the humble dryer back then is a completely different beast today.

Hair dryers have come full circle from the original industry favourite called *Wiggo*, that was sturdy and heavy to hold. Now we have so much more choice with light weight alternatives such as the innovative Dyson brand, to round brush dryers, and every shape, weight, and varying types of technology.

The round brushes favoured back then were called *bottle brushes*. The diameter was very small, about the size of a marker pen. The curl results were very tight, with the volume strong and technically executed. Let me say, those blow-dries lasted a full week! The message here is that by understanding the science and technology behind blow-drying, you'll better create stunning long lasting blow-dries every time.

    Let me give you an example I experienced recently on a photo shoot – I came across a model with strong naturally curly hair. Due to excessive colouring, the ends were damaged and dried very quickly, not allowing enough blow-dry time to control the fuzzy ends. The reason I bring this up is that it was impossible to get the ends of the hair to smooth correctly had I not reapplied a light mist of blow-dry lotion again to the ends, to get a better result. Don't be afraid to re-wet sections, and continue drying to get a better outcome.

    When blow-drying the hair, it must be evenly wet to effectively break the hydrogen bonds down successfully. It also allows for better tension and stretch to achieve a stronger bouncy result.

DIFFERENT TYPES OF BLOW-DRIES

There are many ways to blow-dry hair, and most hairdressers have their own techniques to achieve different blow-dry trends. They have also figured out what brushes and products to use for the different hair types, and generally speaking, can blow-dry and finish all hair types really well. But for some stylists, blow-drying doesn't come easy, so this information is here to help! I've included a list of the most requested blow-dries and tips on how to achieve them.

Straight blow-dry

This image demonstrates the correct blow-dryer angle when drying the hair downwards. The dryer nozzle should always be directed in the same direction the hair falls. This will ensure the heat from the dryer will aid in sealing the cuticle down flat, giving polish and shine to the hair.

This approach creates a sleek and polished look, with a super straight finish and minimal height on the crown, generally with a centre parting.

Depending on the hair type, for example a strong curl that is resistant to change, tension and good stretch is required using the appropriate heat setting to achieve straight hair. Straightening curls is best achieved using a large round bristle brush to give better tension and control when stretching the curl straight. Always angle the hair dryer in a downwards direction from the top of the head for better air control.

Also, it's vital to slow down when blow-drying each section. The slower you move the dryer along the hair, the smoother it will be. Never continue to dry hair when it's already dry as it will dehydrate the hair and cause static.

Taking into consideration the importance of changing the internal structure to reform the hydrogen bonds, the hair must be wet thoroughly to achieve a perfectly straight finish. For hair with minimal curl, a paddle brush or a large barrel round brush can be used. The sleek straight blow-dry looks best on hair with longer layers.

Round brush volume

This image illustrates a volume blow-dry and the brush placement during a volume drying process.

This is considered the most popular service in salons today. It's a classic bouncy blow-dry that will give lift on the crown and soft flicks with curls gathering together towards the ends of the hair.

To add volume, use your fingers to direct the roots out and allow the air to move upwards while removing excess water from the hair. Once excess water is removed, add mousse or thermal styling products prior to sectioning. Start by dividing the head into four sections, blow-drying one section at a time, and clipping the other sections out of the way.

Depending on the type of curls required, the diameter of the brush base must be considered. Remember this rule: hair must wrap a minimum of twice around the diameter of the brush for maximum curl result.

Begin drying from the top of the head to the nape. Use sections the same width as the diameter of the brush. Begin the process by flat wrapping the hair around the brush at the roots, direct the nozzle at the roots, and once dry, roll the brush out to the ends, followed by heat from the dryer, winding each curled section into a roll, clipped to hold while the hair cools down.

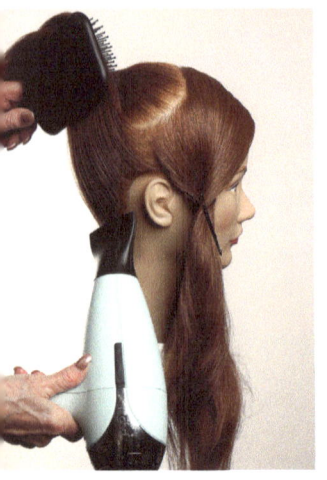

Directional blow-drying

In this image, note the nozzle placement and the angle when doing a directional blow-dry up from the nape to the crown.

This drying technique is used when the finished look calls for definite root direction. A directional blow-dry is the technique of drying the roots in the direction of where the hair will be styled. The direction can be 90 degrees off the scalp for maximum volume, or instead you can choose zero elevation if a sleek flat to the scalp finish is required.

Mostly, I choose a zero-elevation directional dry when wanting to create a sleek polished power ponytail, or if I'm styling the hair flat away from the face, or directing the hair into a tight nape bun.

There are many different 'on trend' looks that warrant a directional blow-dry when preparing the hair.

Let's look at the steps for drying hair into a sleek ponytail as a great example:

Firstly, choosing between a brush or a narrow tooth comb, will determine the degree of flatness at the roots. The comb will get closer to the roots and offer more tension for a flatter result. While a brush will give the root direction, it will not lay as flat to the scalp.

Decide where the pony will be placed, then divide the front section away from the back in line with the back of the ears.

Begin at the back by wetting the root area thoroughly with a thermal styling spray or mousse.

Section a 1 cm wide horizontal parting, beginning at the crown. Comb the hair upwards towards the crown, dry the roots and repeat the above, working section by section to the nape – remember the dryer must always follow the brush closely.

Continue drying the roots at the front, using 1cm wide sections, working from the internal area out to the hairline.

Diffuser dry

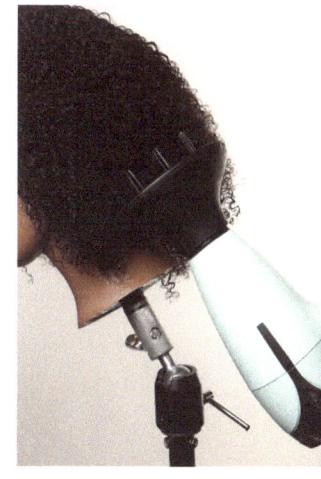

This image shows a bowl diffuser being used to control the airflow and limit the activation of the curls during the drying process.

Diffuser drying is used to enhance natural curl textures. There are many different types of diffusers you can choose from on the market. The most popular ones are a fabric sock style and a plastic bowl style diffuser with small cones inside to ensure heat is distributed evenly without disturbing the curl. Both options attach onto a standard blow-dryer nozzle.

There are definite rules that must be followed to achieve beautiful, diffused curls.

Moisture is key when achieving frizz free curls. When styling curly hair, it is important to remember to keep enough moisture in the hair. Once you've cleansed and conditioned the hair, squeeze dry the hair with your hand, avoiding rubbing the hair with a towel.

It is at this point that styling products are applied. Evenly distribute these into wet hair, using a wet brush or a Denman brush to detangle the hair and evenly distribute the product to form noodle like clumps, allowing the curls to spring back into their individual defined curl formation.

To distribute the product, either section the hair or place the head upside down and apply the product in this fashion. Once the product has been applied to the hair, remove the excess moisture or product with a microfibre towel. It's important to note at this stage of the styling process not to touch the curls while they are drying.

Depending on the end result, some people like to twist curl each section of hair around a finger, working from the bottom to the top of the head for a more separated ringlet curl effect. When using the diffuser, cup each section of hair into the diffuser and hold for 5 seconds. Slowly release and move onto the next section, working your way around the head. Always keep the diffuser moving around the head, drying small sections at a time, and trying not to disturb the curl pattern while diffusing. Use a low heat, cupping the hair into the diffuser, moving it up towards the roots. Once the ends are nearly dry, hover the dryer over the roots to ensure they are also drying at the same pace.

To achieve root lift and voluminous curls, tilt the head upside down. Move the diffuser across the hair for even air flow. Only allow the hair to dry to 80%, in order to leave some moisture in the hair. Don't comb the curls after drying, it will disrupt the natural curl pattern and frizz the hair.

'C' formation blow wave

In this image, note the angle the nozzle is placed inside the 'C' wave formation, and how the comb is holding down the outer edge of the hair in place while drying.

Remember the nozzle always moves across the wave movement in one direction only e.g. with a left side parting, dry the wave from the right side across to left side.

This technique is my all-time favourite when I'm asked to create a classic modern finger wave, and is my go-to trick before beginning to set or tonging. Taking the time to blow wave this movement will make the difference between a beautiful balanced wave, and one that lacks definition.

Firstly, create a left side parting, comb the hair straight back from the forehead, and wet the panel between the outer eyebrows with a thermal spray, making sure the roots are thoroughly wet.

Place the index finger diagonally onto the panel, on the right-hand side, from the middle of the eyebrow, and point the finger towards the side parting on the other side. Hold the finger on the hair firmly in place. Comb the hair behind the finger, swinging the hair across to the corner of the outer eyebrow from left to right.

Use a metal end tail comb carefully placed at the left parting, and section off the panel in a C movement, drawing the tail comb down towards the outer right eye. Carefully section the back area away. Remove your finger and you should have created a 'C' shape movement in the front panel.

The next step is to blow-dry this front section till it is crunchy and dry. Use a nozzle, blow-drying in the opposite direction to where the hair is sitting. For example, if the hair is combed from left to right across the face, then the nozzle must be directed right to left. Once completely dry, brush well and set, tong, or round brush blow-dry the mid lengths and ends.

PRO BLOW-DRYING TIPS

1. Analyse the hair prior to shampooing to assess hair type, porosity, etc.

2. Have a thorough consultation with the client to establish the end result.

3. Shampoo same day for best results.

4. Blast dry 30% of the water from the hair before applying hair sealant, or a porosity equaliser if required.

5. Add styling products to damp hair to avoid diluting the strength of the products.

6. Consider the porosity of the hair, and select the correct blow-dry setting to avoid dehydration.

7. Make sure you choose a dryer that will minimise heat damage to the hair.

8. Remove the blow-dry nozzle when removing the excess water from the hair for an even heat distribution.

9. Use a leave-in conditioner fortified with high moisture protection before drying curly hair.

10. Use a nozzle on the dryer when doing a directional blow-dry.

11. A blow-dry with strong root direction and curl is a great base to create an any up-do.

12. Extreme humidity can be a major factor when a long-lasting blow-dry is required. Use anti-humidity products to help create an invisible shield over the hair.

CHAPTER 9

WAVES

'Pour yourself a cup of ambition.'

– DOLLY PARTON

When I think of glamorous waves, my mind immediately goes back to the 1940s and the sirens of the silver screen, namely Rita Hayworth, Lauren Bacall, and Veronica Lake. These women were revered for their beauty, and applauded for their exceptional Hollywood waves that have stood the test of time.

Their beautiful waves are regularly used as inspiration and featured on mood boards today.

Finger waves have been a styling staple for decades, and continue to evolve with subtle variations. From the tight polished wave formation of the 1940s, leading to today's Hollywood waves which are a much flatter and less defined version.

Comparing the timeline of classic waves, to that of a classic bob cut, both have been part of hair history forever in one form or another. It's how the old classics are interpreted and their constant evolution, that makes these iconic styles still as popular today.

Finger waves are possibly the most challenging to achieve. The traditional waves created through the 1920s–1940s were flat and moulded close to the head with perfectly created crests.

Today vintage or glamour waves are achieved quite differently from the original techniques used, and these days a tong or even a straightener is used to form wave movement, but the results are generally a softer, looser version than the original vintage waves we use as inspiration today.

There are really so many different ways you can create stunning waves. From a twisted round brush blow-dry, to a flat 'S' shape formation with a straightener, to twisted thermal tong sets. The new techniques are endless, creating a modern take on the glamour waves from bygone eras.

Traditional finger waves

The classic moulded finger wave takes a lot of skill and practice. Sadly, this technique is not always taught in trade schools these days, and it has become somewhat of a dying art. If you have a passion to expand your skill set, move into the editorial arena, or create hair for cinema and TV, this traditional skill is important to perfect.

I like to apply a combination of a light moulding crème mixed with gel, which allows the hair to slide into place. Using gel alone can be sticky in the hair and makes it difficult to work with, tugging at the hair. It's best to use a wide tooth cutting comb and to follow the natural wave in the hair. Don't go against the wave, as the wave will not sit well. Waves can be moulded horizontally, vertically, or even diagonally.

It's important to find the natural side parting and begin by combing the hair in a gentle 'C' shape at the part line. Place first two fingers in the middle of the 'C' using pressure to hold, then push the comb below the fingers across the head about 1cm. *Please refer to the image below left.*

Next place the comb flat against the skin and push the comb upwards to form the crest. Reposition the middle finger on top of the teeth of the comb to hold the crest, then place the second finger under the crest, pull the comb out and pinch the fingers together to strengthen the crest. This technique is repeated and continued in alternating directions down to the nape. Keep the waves the same width apart. *Please refer to the image below right.*

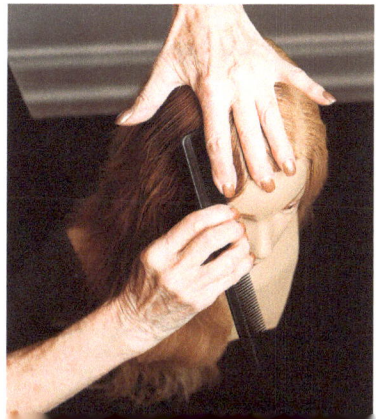
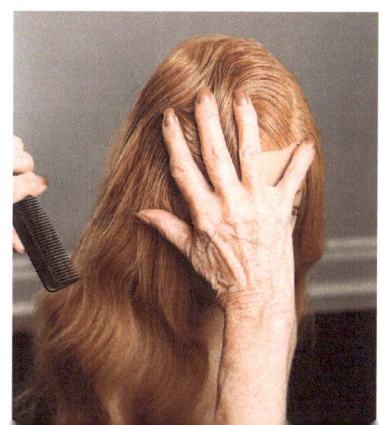

Troughs and crests

To understand waves better, it's important to understand *troughs and crests*, which are the names traditionally given to the wave movement.

The trough is the deepest movement that forms the base of a wave. The crest is the highest point on the top of the wave formation. Think of it like watching rolling ocean waves – the peak of the crest is the highest point at the top of the wave. *You'll see this in the image to the left.*

To create the perfect crest takes enormous skill. The best results are achieved on shorter length hair with uniform layers, preferably with natural wavy hair.

The trick to creating perfect waves is the ability to hold your fingers straight, with strong downward pressure as you direct the comb and hair below. I was taught to bend my wrist and push the palm flat onto the head.

By doing this, it forces your fingers to 'pinch' the crest tightly together, achieving a strong crested wave formation.

From my experience, brushing the waves out after drying sometimes causes the waves to leave a demarcation. If given the choice, I'd prefer not to brush or comb the hair, but leave it in its original form, however this may not always be an option.

Pin curl set

Traditional pin curl setting dates way back, and this technique is recommended when a classic vintage wave movement is desired. The pin curls are set on wet hair, and I suggest adding a medium hold setting lotion to ensure the set has a strong curl result.

I prefer a uniform layered haircut to achieve the perfect wave result. Although this technique can be achieved on longer layers, it is quite difficult to roll excessively long layers into the small pin curls.

Keep in mind that the curls can take up to one hour to dry, hence a drying bonnet attached to the blow dryer will help get the job done.

The most important factor to keep in mind when creating a pin set is knowing what you wish to achieve. In fact, having a strong visual plan is paramount to designing any type of set.

I love using the reverse pin curl method when a beautiful vintage wave is required. The technique requires one row of pin curls set in a clockwise direction, then a row below in an anti-clockwise direction to ensure the wave 'S' shape pattern is strong and well formed. *Please refer to the image to the right.*

Combined with voluminous curls and waves, when brushed out, the results are spectacular and ready for a *Vogue* cover!

Dry pin curls

If time is not on your side, the same setting pattern as the wet set on the previous page can be applied to dry hair, giving a beautiful wave result, but not as long lasting.

Using the same sectioning pattern and curl formation as the wet set, each curl is clamped with a straightening iron, holding it down till the curl is 'pancaked' flat. Clip the curl in place, using a short single prong clip to allow it to cool down. *Please refer to the image at bottom left.*

The dry set gives a modern sexy wave with great curly texture. Remember that this technique can also be used in different sections of the head, namely the front section where a beautiful wave is needed.

Hot roller waves

Soft natural waves can be created after using hot rollers. I suggest 'blow waving' the first movement around the hairline into position, then hot roller setting the mid lengths and ends. *The bottom right image is an example of an 'on-base' application of hot rollers.*

Set the front top section in a 'C' format around the face, beginning at the side parting and curving around to the outer eyebrow on the opposite side. See additional information back in Chapter 8 on the 'C' formation blow wave.

When brushing, make sure you relax the set well. Use the wave clips to strengthen up the movement, alternating with long smooth metal sectioning clips to hold in place. Add a light hairspray and use low speed cool air to dry and set the waves in place.

Wave clips

Metal wave clips can be placed horizontally in a continuous line around the head, holding the crest in place while drying. These clips are perfect when a flat vintage wave result is required. If using any clips, be mindful that they can leave demarcations in the hair, and make sure the teeth of the clip are always straight before placing them in the hair. *Please refer to the images on the left.*

These clips were popular in the early 1920s to help the formation of beautiful flat finger waves. They give the strongest wave formation, especially on wet hair. Wave clips are timeless and come in handy when creating wave definition in many looks today. The secret is to invest in good quality aluminium rust-proof clips with a firm spring coil. They come in various lengths from 3-5 inches.

PRO WAVE TIPS

1. The pin curl set must be completely dry to avoid an uneven curl result.

2. When setting a traditional pin curl, I recommend using a single prong clip to avoid demarcation on the curl.

3. Use the wide end of the cutting comb, not pressing hard on the scalp to avoid scratching.

4. If you wish to explore more detail about setting pin curls, I highly recommend you check out the book: *The Scientific Approach to Hair Design ... Pivot Point System* by Leo Passage and Robert Clegg.

CHAPTER 10

THERMAL SETTING

'It takes five times before you'll perfect a technique, so just start practicing!'

– SHARON BLAIN

Before we start, remember to keep in mind the underpinning knowledge of hair science shared in Chapter 7. To recap, when hair is wet or heated, the hydrogen bonds within the hair structure are temporarily broken down, allowing the natural hair shape to be altered and reformed into the new shape.

Hydrogen bonds are sensitive to heat as well as water. For example, if the hair is exposed to enough humidity, the bonds will break, creating unwanted frizz, or it will revert back to its natural shape.

A straightener or curling tong can quickly and temporarily change the original hair texture when the hydrogen bonds are broken by the heat, and reformed into the new curl or straightened shape.

TENSION, HEAT, AND COOL DOWN

What is tension?

Both tension and stretch are required to alter the shape of the natural texture of the hair. Blow-drying and thermal tong setting require both to break down the hydrogen bonds.

When tong setting, using a fine-tooth comb and a thermal spray will help give better stretch to the hair. Don't allow the hair to be limp when wrapping each section around the tong – you need to have strong tension from roots to the ends. The same principles apply when delivering a bouncy blow-dry.

Best heat

The temperature you choose is vital to achieving long lasting curls. Different hair types need different heat temperatures. With fine, fragile, bleached, and chemically damaged hair, it's vital to lower the heat settings to avoid burning the hair.

Note that the hair cuticle can be damaged when the temperature setting is over 180 degrees.

Imagine a silk shirt that's been burnt with an iron – there is no way to repair the damaged shirt. In the same way, heat can cause irreparable damage to hair, which is why I recommend starting on a lower heat setting to begin with. Test a few curls to see if the results are strong enough. Only increase the heat setting if needed. Following this rule will ensure that the hair will not be compromised.

Cool down

Don't allow your curls to hang down while still hot, the curl will begin to relax too quickly, not giving the bonds time to reform into the new shape. Granted you may wish for a loose soft curl finish, but if you want a long-lasting bouncy curl, then clipping up each curl at the base and allowing it to cool down thoroughly, is the only way to guarantee a perfect result.

Thermal setting

Have you ever wondered why some heads of hair hold curls and others just don't? A major consideration is the science behind the curl process – this is crucial underpinning knowledge. What I discovered to overcome this major challenge, is how the hair needs to '**feel**' for a curl to last.

I've spoken about how the hair should feel when creating any long hairstyle back in Chapter 3. Here is a little reminder – you want to feel '**cotton not silk**'. I just can't say it enough!

A big one for me is making sure the hair has been shampooed the day prior. Hair performs better on the second day due to natural elements and oils in the hair. It allows the hair to develop a grittier rough texture, which gives that 'cotton' like feel, making styling a breeze.

The only time this rule alters is when blow-drying hair. I prefer to blow-dry hair that's freshly shampooed, then layering with the necessary styling products to get the results I'm after.

From there it's the correct choice of products, and learning to layer just enough to get the exact feel you need. Hair types vary and so do the products of choice. I have gone into more detail on this earlier, especially highlighting the specific preparation needed for fine hair.

To recap the art of creating long lasting curls

- Shampoo the day before

- Don't straighten the hair first with a straightener

- Analyse the hair type and features

- Establish the porosity and elasticity of the hair

- Choose the correct product to layer in the hair

- Select the correct tool diameter

- Use a strong thermal setting spray

- Distribute evenly on each section

- Use the correct heat setting

- Use strong tension

- Allow hair to cool

- Spray a light mist of medium hold spray to help set the curl

HOT TOOLS

Prior to Frenchman Marcel Grateau inventing the *Marcel Curling Iron* in 1890, history tells us hot tongs have been used as far back as ancient Egypt to style and dress hair. These primitive implements needed to be heated over a naked flame prior to curling, and the damage to hair was extremely difficult to avoid. With the invention of electricity came thermal tools with temperature-controlled heat settings that we know today, limiting unnecessary damage to the hair.

With today's hair trends, the trusty hot tong is one of the most popular tools used for styling worldwide.

When hot rollers hit the market in the late 1950s, they were a welcome solution to creating voluminous, long-lasting curls on dry hair in a limited time frame. Even today many hairdressers still favour hot rollers as they are quick and reliable.

Along with the introduction of different types of technology, we are spoiled for choice when it comes to hot tongs, stylers, and straightening irons. I have listed below the most popular tools used today, including information on the features and benefits of the different types available.

Conical Tongs

Once you understand the best way to curl with a conical tong, your mind will open up to many possibilities. The cone shaped barrel tong comes in two diameter sizes of 13mm and 19mm, with the thicker area at the handle, tapering down to a smaller diameter with a cold tip end.

The conical tong gives a uniform curl result from roots to ends. Designed to curl longer hair, with dehydrated or difficult to curl ends, the choice of diameter will depend on the desired result.

Here are a few tips – when using a tong without a clamp, make sure the tension is strong and the hair is wrapped evenly for a perfect curl result. When using a conical tong for creating on-trend Hollywood waves, my suggestion is to always wind the curls in the same direction around the head for the best possible outcome. And when using the different diameter tongs in the one head of hair, you can achieve a multi texture dishevelled look.

Hot rollers

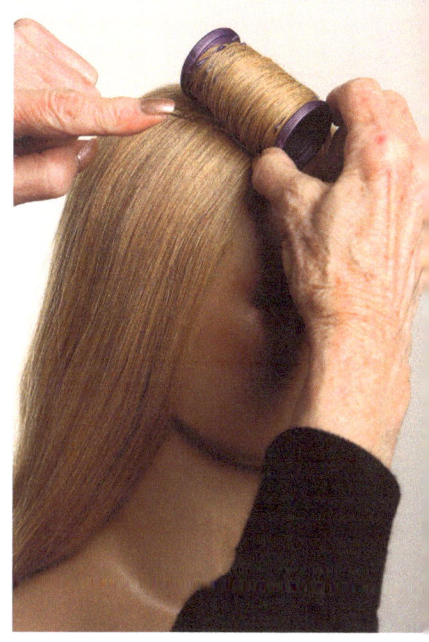

A set of hot rollers comes in various sizes, with different numbers depending on the set, and they are guaranteed to create beautiful bouncy curls of any length and thickness in under an hour! I'm not a fan of hot rollers with the velvet flocking coating as they don't ever feel hot enough. Most hot rollers have a dual temperature setting that heat up in about 5 minutes.

If I had to choose between hot rollers or a barrel tong to get a strong bouncy curl, I'd take the hot rollers any time. The heat from hot rollers is far less than a curling tong, hence kinder on the hair.

The trick is to place the rollers from the crown and work down to the nape. Importantly, the rollers need to be left in the hair till completely cold to get the best result. I recommend adding a light spray of hairspray over the rollers while they are cooling down, especially on finer hair for an extra kick.

Straightening iron

These became popular in the 1980s when the straight hair trend became fashionable. And since the 1990s, women have used them to give their hair a chic, sleek appeal.

The irons are typically made from ceramic, designed to help smooth and temporarily straighten the hair. One of the most impressive features is how the heat from the straightener seals the cuticle, adding shine and sleekness to the hair. The iron can also create a ribbon curl when the hair is wrapped between the plates and pressure applied as you roll the tool, curving it downwards while pulling through to the ends of the hair. More recently we have seen many different types of exciting techniques using the iron, creating various wave patterns and different textures.

Barrel tongs

Spoilt for choice, barrel tongs are available in a variety of styles, with the diameter from as small as a lead pencil, right up to a large 38mm diameter. Tongs are also available in different lengths to suit different lengths of hair. Check out tongs with changeable varying barrel sizes and shapes for a cost-effective option. Consider purchasing a tong with a finger control lever, and I also recommend one with a cool tip at the end as it's much easier to use.

Elevate Pro Styler

I couldn't finish this chapter without mentioning my very first hot tool – The Elevate Pro Styler. It's a unique addition to the hot tool range and a quick simple styling solution that adds airy volume at the roots as well as creating soft curls, beachy textures, and smooths the hair. It creates long-lasting volume and texture in the hair minimising the need for teasing or products. Used only on dry hair, it comes with a choice of three heat settings from 140-180 degrees for different hair types and porosity.

An important feature of the Elevate Pro and why I put my name to it is that it will not 'flatten' the hair, hence you'll be able to maximise body and bounce. My favourite way to use it is to create texture at the roots, and then set the ends with hot rollers or a tong to create incredible volume and movement on any hair type.

CHAPTER 11

STYLING HACKS

'Great things are done by a series of small things brought together.'

– VINCENT VAN GOGH

In the previous chapters I've covered my best tips and knowledge to assist you in creating fabulous hair.

As a hairdresser of 50+ years, I've spent years experimenting, exploring, learning, and perfecting different ways to pin, tease, sew or set, and I've road tested so many different alternatives to simplify the art of dressing hair.

Often the 'old school' methods of hair styling have proven to be the best, and dare I say it, are foolproof. However, with changing hair trends and limited timeframes, sometimes these methods need shaking up, which fuels an innate curiosity in me to improve and simplify techniques wherever I can!

I'm 'unlocking' the information in this chapter to help make complicated techniques less complex, so you can get on with creating beautiful finished looks you might have previously felt were impossible!

PINNING HAIR

Make sure you use strong good quality bobby pins that lock in securely and hold the heaviest hair in place. There are many different ways to place a pin in hair. The end result is making sure the pins hold the hair in place, and are well hidden.

A most contentious and commonly asked question is 'do the ridges face up or down when pinning'? I prefer the ridge facing up. The main reason I say this is due to the tip of the pin - the top is shorter and curves upwards, while the bottom is slightly longer. When placing a pin with the ridges upwards, the long length slides better under the layers at the roots, and grips more securely.

Cross pin

How many times do you place pins into your up-do, only to find no matter how many pins you use, it's just not holding? There's a good reason for this. You need to understand the flow of the hair.

To dive a little deeper, imagine the hair is flowing horizontally at the side of the head, into a high pony. The pins won't hold if you try pinning into the layers by angling the pin in a horizontal direction towards the pony. This is because there is nothing for the pin to grip into.

Alternatively, placing that same pin in a vertical direction allows the pin to lock into the hair as the horizontal layers allow the pin to catch and grip. The key message here: always check the direction of the hair at the base, and pin across the direction to hold securely. *Please refer to the image on the left.*

Criss-cross pinning

I recommend criss-crossing pins for a strong hold. Additionally, If you are adding hair padding or wefts, this will give an even stronger hold.

I suggest creating a narrow scalp braid at the roots in the region where the pins will be attached. Then pin through into the braid with the criss-cross method. I guarantee nothing will move! *Please refer to the image on the left.*

Weave pinning

This is a great way to disguise pins in very soft loose textures. Firstly, I prefer to use shorter length pins as opposed to regular pins, as they weigh the texture down too much. And it's much easier to hide shorter pins with multi-textured looks.

Begin by selecting the section of hair to be pinned, open the pin, and slip it over the edge of the section. Close the pin, then create a weaving pattern with the pin down into the hair. Flip the pin over and downwards, latching into the layers of hair below to secure the section. *Please refer to the images.*

Latch pinning

Often when creating a hairstyle with soft pulled out pieces on the crown for example, it looks great until you have to pin. Unless you're super careful, the pins will take away the beautiful look. My preference is using a latch pin. Take a very small elastic band with two bobby pins attached. Slip one pin into the side of the section on the left and stretch the elastic carefully across the centre panel, then slip the second pin into the base of the right-hand section. *See the image in the circle.*

Latch pin tip: I rarely open a bobby pin when pinning hair as it becomes impossible to conceal the top of the pin. The latch pinning technique begins by directing the pin 90% into the hair, pushing towards the scalp, then as the pin touches the skin, flipping the pin under the layers to secure. It's like an 'L' shaped angle.

Latch hook

I first used a latch hook to make a shag pile rug which was very trendy in the 1970s! The hook isn't much different to a crochet hook except it has a small latch over the hook loop that opens and closes.

Some time ago, I was planning to do a Mohawk look for a Hair Expo show.

My idea for the look was to create 6 separate ponytails spaced a few centimetres apart in a vertical line. I wanted to shift each ponytail from its base towards the crown, to the base of the tail above. I didn't want to use bobby pins to secure them. I wanted a clean seamless over direction with the pony. I started playing with the latch hook, and found I was onto something!

I was able to knot an elastic band using the hook under the hair layers, while at the same time securing the tails firmly at the base. The idea was a winner and since then I've continued to use the latch hook in many different applications, and I've sold thousands to hairdressers as a handy tool of the trade.

Let me give you a more technical explanation of why this crafty gadget is so good. Remember the famous classic Audrey Hepburn crown chignon? One of the steps is to direct the hair forward and add a row of criss-cross bobby pins behind the base to secure the hair in place. What tends to happen, when the hair is flipped back over the row of pins, is that the pins then lift off the head and rarely is it smooth or clean, and sometimes the pins can be seen at the base. This is where the latch hook comes in.

To achieve this style, substitute the latching technique and you'll find pinning isn't needed. The section is over-directed and held together with an elastic band and one bobby pin. The best thing with this approach is that the hair falls perfectly back into a stunning fan shape when brushed back.

The latch hook is also fantastic to weave cords into braids, hold cornrows in place, and it's also amazing for attaching various types of hairpieces into the hair without having to pin them into place. *The images on this page help illustrate how I use the latch hook.*

HAIR SEWING

Sewing is my go-to technique to secure hair.

From sewing in finger waves, attaching an avant-garde hairpiece or hair weft, or when creating dishevelled texture up-do's. This is a fun application that's guaranteed to hold until the thread is cut out.

The sewing needles used range from curved metal needles, plastic wool needles, and a variety of different length needles with blunt ends. There is pretty much a needle to suit whatever you are trying to achieve.

When it comes to thread, you can either go for a clear nylon thread (great for blonde hair) that can't be seen, right through to a heavy linen cotton thread, perfect to secure a heavy wire base and hairpieces. Sometimes a fine fishing line comes in handy when strength along with a clear 'unseen' thread is needed.

I can't begin to count how many looks I've sewn together instead of using pins. Here's a tip when working with dancers for example, and there is the real fear of pins falling out when they twist and turn. Sew the looks together and they will stay put and last longer.

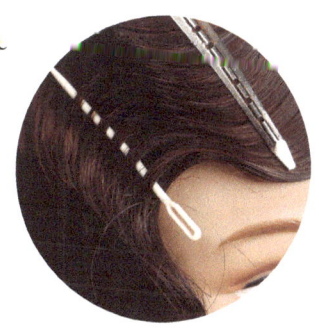

I'm particularly proud of the way I secure my beautiful classic finger waves with a plastic needle and clear thread. Note that you'll probably need a magnifying glass to see the thread! When I use pins to hold sculptured waves in place, it's very difficult to disguise the pins. There is no better trick I know that will secure the wave in place without distorting the wave or seeing the pin. *Please refer to the image to the right.*

Give it a go, it does take practice to perfect sewing waves, but once you master the technique you will never use another pin again!

PADDING

Padding has been used for centuries, and once upon a time horsehair pads, matted rats, and wireframes formed the basis of the grand Edwardian styles and so many other period looks. *Please refer to the image to the left.*

There are many different padding shapes available, made from various materials such as yak, synthetic textured hair, and coarse nylon fibre.

Today the most commonly used shape is the coarse nylon donut, generally added around a pony base to form a classic ballet bun or soft textured shape. I use padding to create a big volume shape to various hairstyles, or for adding shape to the base of finer hair to give the illusion of fullness.

It's vital to always consider the integrity of the hair when styling by avoiding excessive teasing and harsh products where possible. With this in mind, some years back I created a range of padding shapes made from synthetic hair. There are four different shapes and two different colours (blonde and medium brown), to give fullness where needed and to minimise the need to tease the hair. The padding blends perfectly with natural hair and is super lightweight to use.

Below are the padding shapes I've created, with some of the ways I use each one:

The Crescent

Approx. 18cm in length, it's great as a foundation for a small nape chignon, or for adding height and fullness where needed.

Cone padding

The cone is 15cm long and shaped similar to a French roll, wider at the top and tapering down at the bottom.

Oblong padding

Approx. 20cm long x 8cm wide with square ends. This is my favourite go-to shape due to its flexibility to achieve any imaginable shape.

Round padding

10cm wide, this traditional donut shape is suitable as a base for textured buns and adding volume to classic ballet buns.

When it comes to pinning padding, rule number one is that it must be secure. The trick is to follow the rules on how to pin, as detailed earlier.

Secondly, to pin the padding, first check the direction the hair is flowing at the base, place the pin through the edge of the padding, then into the hair base below, remembering to pin across the base to lock and secure.

And lastly, when planning to create a large shape, add multiple pieces of padding together until you form the desired shape. Either pin or sew the pieces together for a firm foundation.

BRUSHING

In the following notes, I've referred to the word 'setting' throughout to keep things simple. Keep in mind **setting** refers to wet sets, hot roller sets, tong setting, and round brush blow-drying.

Never be afraid to brush the hair thoroughly after curling. I'm aware some will be concerned the set will not last if brushed, but if you've done a beautiful set and allowed it to cool down long enough and used the correct products for the hair type, there should be no cause for concern.

Brushing helps to break up the curls and blend the sections together, whilst allowing you to see exactly how the hair will sit. I prefer to use a paddle brush on long hair to make sure the entire head is brushed from roots to ends, not just the surface of the hair.

I know of hairdressers who love using the *Mason Pearson* brush with its combination of boar and nylon bristles. And after using the paddle, generally I swap to a similar type of brush to finish off and mould the hair into place.

Dry hair moulding is a term used when brushing the hair into the original setting pattern, or brushing the hair into the way you want the design to look.

When brushing a herringbone set for example, it's important to brush out the hair in the direction the hair was originally set to help enhance the wave formation. *Please refer to the images below.*

PRO BRUSHING TIPS

1. It's great to brush against the roots in the opposite direction to the set for extreme volume.

2. Brushing the hair in different directions from the roots to the ends, then moulding back to its original form, really helps determine how the hair is going to respond and avoid static.

3. 'Instagram' style curls are generally combed through with an extra wide tooth comb or paddle sized vent brush, giving a more dishevelled loose undone vibe.

4. Begin brushing the hair out at the same spot you began originally setting the hair.

5. If the hair is inclined to be oily, limit the amount of brushing to avoid the set dropping and relaxing.

TEASING

Teasing is also known as back-combing. Essentially it is knotting or matting the hair using a narrow tooth comb, brush, or teasing comb. It is most effectively achieved on hair that has been well prepared prior.

Over time, I have developed a standard set of teasing rules and where to apply the different types of teasing to achieve the best styling results.

To help understand better, I teach different techniques, from using your fingers, a brush, or a comb, and how each technique delivers a very different result and outcome.

Teasing is not a case of one size fits all. Using your fingers will give a soft pop of loose texture, the brush a more cobweb texture, and the comb will build an extra strong root foundation for maximum height.

A tip when attempting to tease heavy or slippery hair texture, is using a light dusting of texture powder or a light mist of hairspray at the roots to help give the hair more grip and making it easier to tease well.

Texture teasing

When you require a soft light texture, for example in a straighter down style, or you wish to add a little bit of a dishevelled vibe to a down wave or a curl, texture teasing is the best option. I like to use my fingers to achieve this as you can *see in the images below.*

Catch the section of the hair to be softened and run it between two fingers. Tightly pinch the fingers together and push the fingers up against the natural fall of the hair. You will notice the hair texture fluff up and become airy. It's better to use fingers for this purpose to avoid a defined stop start demarcation line that happens when using a comb or brush.

Brush teasing

Back brushing is designed to achieve airy teasing and height at the roots. When using a brush to tease, the results are more cobweb-like without a strong structural texture. The cobweb texture is perfect to add volume and makes it easy to smooth the outer surface of the shape. *Please refer to the images below.*

I use this teasing technique when creating self-padding within a hairstyle. Let me explain – say that I'm working with excessively thick hair and the brief is for a large chignon shape, where a padding piece is generally added to create the base of the chignon. With thick hair I recommend working from a pony base, dividing the pony into two sections, then using the underneath section for the padding and the top section to smooth over the padding shape. Consider adding a fine hair net around the teased section to control and form the desired chignon shape.

Matting

I like to use this technique when I want to hold a panel of hair together, so it doesn't fall apart or separate. Using a narrow tooth comb and beginning at the underside of the section, start a centimetre out from the roots. Push the comb towards the roots and continue down the section leaving one-centimetre distance between each movement before pushing the comb towards the roots. Always make sure the matting doesn't show on the outer surface. *Please refer to the image on the left.*

Remember the angle you hold the hair is also important, for example, when trying to hold a shoulder length bob together at the ends, the hair should be held at 0 degrees to ensure the shape holds together well.

Comb teasing

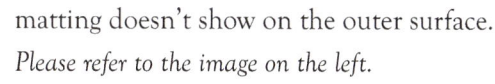

When looking to create excess height with maximum strength at the base, I always use a fine-tooth comb, and make sure the hair is well brushed and tangle free before beginning.

Hold each section taut and tease the underside, pushing the comb with a slight forward curved motion down towards the roots and repeat with three light strokes.

Use short strokes to form a strong powerful root structure. Add a light hairspray at the roots for extra hold. This technique is my go-to when I'm creating a huge shape that will stand 90 degrees off the head. It allows the hair to hold strong due to this strong teasing. *Please refer to image on the left.*

PRO TEASING TIPS

1. Hold your section at 90 degrees out from the head when teasing with a comb for maximum height.

2. Only tease from the roots out to the height desired. Preserve the quality of the hair and avoid teasing the mid-lengths to ends of the hair if not needed.

3. The action of teasing starts approx. 2cm from the scalp.

4. Take a section approx. 1cm deep, and no wider that the tool being used.

5. Select a section, make short pulsing movements at the roots with a narrow tooth comb, building up the texture. Then pack the stacking down to the scalp. Place the comb 1cm above the packing and begin stacking again. I call this the 'Stack and Pack' method!

6. Add texture powder or hair spray at the roots if the hair is difficult to tease.

PONYTAILS

The main message about ponytails is the importance of doing a directional blow-dry prior if you require a nice sleek finish. Refer to the chapter on blow-drying for more information. I suggest breaking the hair into two sections when adding the band. It's easier to keep stronger tension and control of the hair. Working at the back first, divide the back off from the front behind the ears, placing a band into this section. Once secured, add the remaining front section to the back pony and band both together.

Try using a regular elastic band with two bobby pins attached when doing a pony base. Simply hold the pony firmly with your hand and slip one pin into the side of the pony. Stretch the band across and around the pony till it is super tight and holds securely, then pop the second pin into the base to hold. Using a band in this way will not tangle or damage the hair and will be easier to remove.

I often use hat elastic to secure a ponytail – the downside is it requires two people, one to hold and one to tie. I refer to this method as a runway ponytail technique. I would recommend this option when requiring the tightest sleek pony possible. This pony is often said to give a mini face lift at the same time due to how tight you can get it.

With this application, there are four sections, beginning with a narrow back panel, and the front is broken down into three sections. The middle front section allows flexibility to offer a variation, by adding height, texture, or even a braid if desired. *Please refer to the images below.*

The final piece of valuable information I must share, refers to the placement of the pony on the top of the head and how to actually find the top of the head.

Everyone has a different shaped scalp, so giving a set of measurements of how to find the exact 'spot' won't work for everyone. The simplest way to find the top of the head is making sure your client sits up straight, looking forward. Then placing a comb on top of the head, running from the forehead to the crown, allow the comb to overhang at the crown. Imagine the comb is a spirit level – the comb must sit flat on the head without tilting.

Immediately below the point where the head curves and the comb leaves the head, is the top of the head for this person. I would recommend using this test when you need to establish the top prior to cutting, as well as when planning a style with a design that needs to be seen from the front.

HAIR NETS

Many years ago, I saw an incredible hair show in Paris presented by the famous *Alexandre De Paris*. He was the master of dressing stunning classic long hair, and I credit him as one of the inspirational artists I most identify with today.

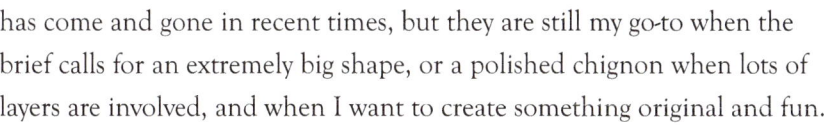

He worked a lot with very fine hair nets, covering long sections of hair with the nets, then moulding and shaping this into stunning designs.

The use of hair nets in long hair styling has come and gone in recent times, but they are still my go-to when the brief calls for an extremely big shape, or a polished chignon when lots of layers are involved, and when I want to create something original and fun.

There are a few different types of nets on the market. A very small bun net is great to hold a tight ballet bun together. A regular size net can cover most sized heads which makes it my go-to size for most of the creative work I do. Then there is an extra-long net, great for when braiding extremely long hair and doing avant-garde pieces.

The nets are super fine, very delicate, and become invisible in the hair. They need to be treated very carefully as it's possible to make a hole in them quite easily. They come in all different shades from white to black and many colours in between. *Please refer to the images below.*

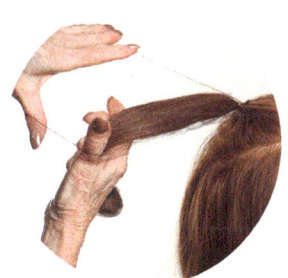
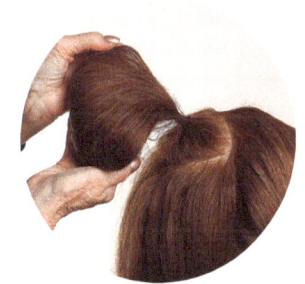

PRO HAIR NET TIPS

1. I often colour the white nets using food colouring as a contrast in the hair for a more editorial look.

2. Other times I'll use nets over very heavy braids that coil around the head. Once pinned well, I then make small holes here and there in the net, pulling loops of hair through the holes for a more textured loose dishevelled look.

3. The best way to hold a low polished chignon is to use a net to secure it in place.

4. Working with super thick hair? Try pinning a net around the base of a ponytail, then twisting both the hair and net together. Wrap the twist into a neat bun down on the head and pin.

PRODUCT HACKS

A big no-no is overusing styling products, especially hair spray. The plastic unnatural finish from over spraying hair also changes the colour tone making it appear dull and lifeless.

As an alternative during the styling process, I recommend using a combination of medium hold hairspray and weightless shine spray. The shine will help control unruly frizz, while at the same time helps avoid plastic build up from the hair spray.

To help correct oily roots, try spraying the root area with hair spray to absorb the oil.

To break down the build-up of hair spray, lightly spray the over sprayed area with a weightless shine spray, allow it to sit for ten seconds, then watch the hair spray evaporate. This makes it easy to rework the hair again. Alternatively, if you have used to much oil, add a light mist of hair spray to counteract the oil.

STRAIGHTENER USE

I've mentioned this before – but I'm going to remind you, DO NOT use a straightener prior to styling hair! To fully understand the reasoning, we need to consider that the geometric shape of the hair fibres is affected when a straightener is used.

The hot plates of a straightener squash the hair fibre into a flat pancake shape. This makes the hair look flat like sateen ribbon, and makes it impossible to achieve long-lasting curls or textures with most hair types. When using a straightener, I have previously shared how I liken the results similar to working with a piece of fine cardboard – it's difficult to manipulate, and hard to get it to hold a shape. Just because a straightener is easy to use doesn't mean it suits all hair types.

CHAPTER 12

FASHION AND HISTORY

'Clothes ain't going to change the world.

The women who wear them are.'

– ANNE KLEIN

When it comes to hair styling, don't underestimate the importance of learning from the past to help create the future.

Looking back at trends from the different eras, there is a distinct association between fashion and society with modernisation and technology playing a huge role in influencing social behaviours.

The word 'fashion' is not just confined to clothing and accessories, it also includes art, architecture, interiors, hair, beauty, food, and lifestyle. Fashion is a form of expression of who we are, and it gives us the opportunity to shape our identity and influence our lifestyle.

There is so much to understand about history, especially when recreating hairstyles from a particular era. Hair trends from the 1920s through to the 1990s tend to be the most inspirational looks referenced today, and these eras are easily interpreted into more contemporary and relatable styles.

As hair trends continue to be reinvented, I regularly see a subtle nod to the past eras in many of the most popular looks today.

Let's take Farrah Fawcett's curtain fringe and side flicks as a great example – the reinvented version this time around is less constructed and looser in its form, but it's quite apparent there's still a strong Farrah influence.

The bob is another great example of a trend made popular in the 1920s that has continued to reinvent itself over the past 100 years. It's clear the bob sends a message of empowerment and a symbol of feminist fashion, and this can be witnessed in its continued revival.

It did however lose its popularity for a short period of time prior to the 1960s, until Vidal Sassoon gave it a modern makeover. The silhouette of the bob cut has varied in different lengths from long to short over the years, and there have also been style variations from an a-line to textured, inverted, and box bob versions. I can't think of any 'one' hair trend that has persisted as long and been worn by so many.

After doing a deep dive into the history of fashion, I uncovered some interesting facts and trivia that are not only fascinating, but they've helped me better understand how different trends are impacted by various historical events, and how society and culture continues to evolve fashion.

PERIOD HAIR STYLING

Technically speaking, the term 'period hair styling' refers to the centuries between the 1600-1800s.

The evolution of hair variations throughout this period has been extreme to say the least! The complexity of these extreme looks, not to mention the challenge of wearing them, is almost inconceivable. Just imagine having to create these looks without the modern electrical tools and fantastic products we have at our disposal today.

The period movies and series such as *Jane Eyre*, *Marie Antoinette*, *Bridgerton*, and *Elizabeth* are perfect examples of how skilled hair teams are at recreating the hair looks for these periods. I salute the incredibly talented wig makers and hairdressers who spend hours delivering this exceptional reimagined hair. What's extremely hard to even comprehend is that women in these eras wore their hair styled in this fashion on a daily basis, compared to the simplicity of hair styling today.

15th – 16th CENTURY

This period is referred to as the Renaissance period. Hair was worn big, adorned with elaborate hairpieces, coils, and braids.

In this period foreheads were high, and some women even plucked the hair in this area to give an exaggerated look – the high hairline was considered regal. The bright red tint of Titian, along with saffron and gold colour tones were popular. The hairstyles were adorned with pure gold, stunning gems, and pearls.

17th CENTURY

In this period the 'fontange' high headdress was popular. The hair was piled in curls on top of the head and arranged around the headdress in a decorative design. Wire cages and false pieces created the structure for these hair designs. Incidentally, this hair trend evolved by sheer accident. The Duchesse de Fontange (a mistress of Louis XIV) lost her cap while hunting with the king, so she piled up her hair and tied it with ribbon. The king loved the style so much she continued to replicate it, in turn influencing the women of the time who copied her.

Over time the fontange style used more and more elaborate wire structures to support the extreme height and decorative adornment. These elaborate designs lasted until the early 18th century.

18th CENTURY

As time moved through the centuries, hair height became lower. Styles became less structured, with curls or waves covering the forehead and worn above the ears with very little height.

Soft curls and braids were pinned around the nape and draped over the shoulders, with the style adorned using headbands and ribbons. Hair powder became popular at this time, firstly to add a grey tone or whiten the hair, but mainly it was used for hygiene reasons. The type of wigs and pieces used often caused the scalp to become sore and itchy and it's thought the powder helped to absorb oil and avoid infection as well.

19th CENTURY

The Victorian era was born during the reign of Queen Victoria.

There was a trend for women to grow their hair exceptionally long, worn down and flowing. Historic photos show examples of hair as long as the thighs! Setting the hair in rags, curls, or braids overnight was popular, creating a soft wavy texture.

Having extra-long hair made it easier for the hair to be rolled up in a less elaborate way, and pinned on the head for a softer look. For an alternate style, chignons were created on top of the head with tussled curls around the shape, and long ringlets or 'barely there' curls sitting around the face.

20th CENTURY

The different hair variations throughout this period cover all possible options. The whimsical fluffy bouffant famously known as the *Gibson Girl*, kicked off the 20th century before the transition to short bobs and waves. Afro perms, Vidal Sassoon cuts, punk rocker styles, boho and big hair – this is just a sprinkling of all the different hair options that were put to the test and worn loud and proud. Here is a small snapshot of the 20th century:

1920s

Known as the roaring twenties, this period was impacted by World War I and the Spanish flu. The advancement in technology saw the introduction of cars, radio, and telephone, and travel opened the door to unprecedented work and financial freedom. Women won the right to vote, and the *flappers* emerged.

Clothing: dresses were knee length, loose fitting, and embellished with sequins and beads.
Makeup: heavy dark eyes, pale skin, rouge cheeks and cupid bow lips.
Hair: short shingled, straight, and wavy bobs, androgynous hair such as the Eton crop, and boyish slick downs.
Music/Dance: Jazz was all the rage, dances such as the Charleston and Black Bottom became popular.
Icons of the decade: Coco Chanel, Clara Bow, Louise Brooks, Josephine Baker.

1930s

The Great Depression stretched through this decade, with the biggest ever drop in the economy globally. Women became more resourceful, including sewing their own clothing, and the economic climate influenced the type of clothing worn, as fabric was limited in supply.

As a result of the Depression, escapism was through films, and the glamorous sirens of Hollywood's silver screen played a huge role in influencing hair styling, fashion, and makeup during this period.

Fashion: sleek feminine, longer length dresses, waisted and bias-cut frocks.
Makeup: less dramatic eye makeup with various red/coral lip tones.
Hair: beautiful waves, bobs were still in fashion – however some wore it longer to the shoulders with soft fluffy curls around the ends.
Music/dance: jive, swing, and big bands.
Icons of the decade: Jean Harlow, Greta Garbo, Bette Davis, and Joan Crawford.

1940s

World War II extended into the first part of this decade and had a profound effect. While men were fighting for their countries, women took on roles in factories, farms, hospitals, industry, and work associated with the war effort. There was rationing not only for food, but also makeup, stockings, and luxury items – this led to household concoctions that were often used to replace cosmetics.

Fashion: the 'new silhouette' trend, suits, straight knee length skirts, shirtwaist dresses.
Makeup: fuller red lips, clear skin, and pencil eyebrows comprised the look for the decade.

Hair: glamour Hollywood waves, the page boy curl, and pin sets. The Victory Roll, worn at the nape or rolled towards the face was a patriotic symbol of strength during this period. It stood for the victory of being alive each day.
Music/dance: mambo, swing, jazz, and blues.
Icons of the decade: Marilyn Monroe, Grace Kelly, Rita Hayworth, and Katherine Hepburn.

1950s

With the war over, the economy was improving. Rapid changes were seen more in this period than in the past two decades. Times were gentler, and the consumer revolution was about to start in a big way. Both television and the Diners Club Card were introduced, and makeup products like Revlon boomed. Overall, there were more choices than ever before. Fashion designers were making their mark, and rockabilly took over the fashion trends. Hats became very popular.

Fashion: dresses become fuller, bust lines more accentuated with small, cinched waistlines.
Makeup: winged 'cat eye' liner, heavy eyebrow, false eyelashes.
Hair: bouffant set, teased to create fullness, popularity of the pixie and poodle cut.
Music/dance: rock and roll, jive, and cha cha.
Icons of the decade: Audrey Hepburn, Sophia Loren, Elizabeth Taylor, and James Dean.

1960s

Another huge decade of change – the Vietnam war sparked student protests and man walked on the moon. Pop music had a strong influence on hair and fashion trends. The changing social attitudes led to a new form of freedom, mainly in the way young people expressed themselves with hair, fashion, and makeup. Woodstock made its stamp and psychedelic clothes with bright colours and geometric patterns ruled. It was a time of defining lifestyle moments where rockers, hippies, and surfers revolutionised free thinking.

Fashion: Mod fashion, miniskirts, crochet dresses, tie-dyed caftans.
Makeup: more colourful eye makeup, false eyelashes, and pale pink lips.
Hair: Sassoon pixie cut, five-point cut, French roll and beehives, men wore long hair.
Music/dance: The Beatles, The Rolling Stones, locking and popping.
Icons of the decade: Mary Quant, Jacqueline Kennedy, and Brigitte Bardot.

1970s

This period saw double digit inflation marked with huge cultural changes, the questioning of traditional authority, and the fight for women's rights – self-expression and liberation was at its peak. Platform shoes got higher, during what was known as the polyester decade. Discos and nightclubs were all the rage and people wore what they wanted, how they wanted to wear it, with comfort and originality the key.

Fashion: bell bottoms, maxi dresses, ponchos, platform shoes, polyester.
Makeup: lip gloss, shiny blushes, over plucked eyebrows, natural glow makeup.
Hair: mullet, punk, bleached hair, geometric cuts, the shag, the wedge, the Purdy cut.
Music/dance: Motown, disco.
Icons of the decade: Farrah Fawcett, Bianca Jagger, Jerry Hall, and Twiggy.

1980s

This was the era of excess where 'Go Big or Go Home' was the catch cry and there was huge growth in the global population. It was considered the boldest decade in modern fashion history. Materialism and consumerism saw the rise of 'yuppies'. IBM released the first personal computer, while scientists started to recognise global warming issues, and the Berlin Wall came down. Video games, MTV, and blockbuster movies hit the market.

Fashion: shoulder pads, power suits, over the top silhouettes, leg warmers, spandex.
Makeup: clashing colour eye shadows, blue eyeliner, nude lips.
Hair: big hair, spiral perms, bright hair colours, shaves and undercuts, spikes, extensions.
Music/dance: hard rock, hip-hop, country music.
Icons of the decade: Michael Jackson, Madonna, Boy George and Diana, Princess of Wales.

1990s

Often referred to as 'The Good Decade', this era is also remembered as the decade of relative peace and prosperity. The economy began to boom after the end of the early 1990s recession. This era saw the death of Princess Diana and Kurt Cobain, the birth of casual Fridays, the explosion of the World Wide Web, and the huge popularity of TV sitcom *Friends*. 76 million Tamagotchis were sold, and other hot ticket items included the Nokia 3210, roller blades, Nintendo, and Pokémon cards.

Fashion: flares, platform shoes, halter tops, cropped tanks, leather pants, hoodies, bum bags, Doc Martens, baseball caps and grunge.

Makeup: eye colour palette of burgundy, brown blue, matt lipstick in dark tones, thin eyebrows, spider lashes, frosted glitter shadows and lips.

Hair: The Pixie, the Rachel, mullets and gelled spikes, pigtails, braids, crimping, and the big accessory hit – the scrunchie!

Music/dance: Pop culture, hip-hop, rap, the Macarena.

Icons of the decade: Brad Pitt, Janet Jackson, Kate Moss, Naomi Campbell and Jennifer Aniston.

I could fill a book just on the history of hair throughout the decades, and I've included this snapshot down memory lane to get you thinking and encourage your own exploration. It will help you develop a greater understanding of how fashion and style influence each period. It's only then you'll be able to appreciate how hair continues to reinvent itself with references to past trends.

CHAPTER 13

THOUGHT-PROVOKING AVANT-GARDE

'Creativity is contagious. Pass it on.'

– ALBERT EINSTEIN

It's time to take your knowledge, vision, and creativity in a new direction. To take a deep dive into the world of avant-garde and the aspirational styling aspect of the craft.

In the dictionary, the meaning of avant-garde is:

> **'favouring or introducing new and experimental ideas and methods.'**

Avant-garde styling is normally thought of and considered to be ahead of its time. It's generally bold, always innovative, progressive, with experimental characteristics.

Avant-garde is art that is expressed in many different types of mediums, from jewellery design, sculptures, architecture, fashion, makeup, and of course, hair. It's all about risk taking and going beyond what is considered normal.

In the hairdressing world we speak about avant-garde as the extreme end of the styling spectrum. I personally see avant-garde as more *aspirational* hairdressing. That way it becomes more expansive and inclusive of session or editorial styling. The best way to understand the difference between commercial styling that's done on a daily basis in salons today versus the aspirational side of styling, is to think of 'ready to wear' fashion as commercial styling, while haute-couture designer fashion is the avant-garde or the aspirational styling end of the range.

Why is inspiration important to an artist?

Aspirational hair offers less design constraints compared to commercial styling. It opens the door to a new level of inspired creativity. When it comes to avant-garde, we can push the boundaries and truly express ourselves, not dissimilar to painting styles such as abstract, surrealism, and expressionism.

Where does inspiration come from?

Be it art or architecture, nature and environment, fashion, photography, history, movies, a beautiful design, even paint cracking on a wall, or a person's thought-provoking words, inspiration of all kinds flicks a switch between your imagination and soul that might not have been otherwise accessible. It could even be a dream that you wake from, feeling excited about the ideas it inspires.

Exploring creative channels for inspiration

You'll know when that one unique inspirational idea strikes a chord. It could be just one idea that ignites a feeling of strong connection, and can send the heart rate soaring, eyes popping, and the mind going into a tailspin. Your imagination begins to take over, and your creative journey is about to begin. Exploring what's possible, your visualisation takes your mind in a new direction.

The next stage is how to expand that idea into an avant-garde hair collection. Maybe you're planning a show-stopping hair show, shooting a fabulous colour collection, or looking to take your skills in a new direction. For whatever reason, the most important thing is your creative and artistic growth.

I like to set aside time to research various creative channels to aid in establishing my new direction for the next artistic project. I've included below a host of recommendations, my favourite artists from different mediums, and loads of questions and suggestions to explore all available options. I hope these recommendations take you down a 'rabbit hole' and open your eyes to exciting creative possibilities.

Don't forget to screenshot or save any ideas that excite you along the way. Remember, this is the beginning of a glorious journey.

Fashionistas, fashion designers, and music

It could be that you're inspired by renowned fashionistas and fashion designers... Research these few suggestions, but don't limit yourself: **Isabella Blow, Coco Chanel, Jacqueline Kennedy, Dame Vivienne Westwood, Alexander McQueen** and **Baz Luhrmann** are just some of my favourites to get you started.

Isabella Blow

A talented fashion magazine editor for *Tatler*, her fashion styling would uniquely emulate and draw influence from her intense passion for art and history. Izzie, as she was best known, had a remarkable sense of what the next big thing would be. Breathing life into 'up and coming' fashion talents, such as Alexander McQueen (fashion designer) and Philip Treacy (milliner), her signature staple was wearing outlandish hats designed and made by Treacy. She was a vanguard of fashion, flamboyant in nature, and incredibly creative. She was loved by many and died too soon.

As a hairstylist, the history of hair and fashion has strongly influenced me when looking to create new collections. This is why I've been drawn to Isabella's body of work as a fashion director. She exudes a quirky but totally timeless edge that I love.

> 'Dressing without a hat was like not being dressed at all.'
> - ISABELLA BLOW

Jacqueline Bouvier Kennedy Onassis

Jacqueline Bouvier Kennedy Onassis was the most certified style icon of the 1960s and 1970s, and undeniably one of the greatest fashionistas of the last century.

She set many major trends of the era – from the oversized sunglasses, the Chanel box jacket suiting, the polarising pillbox hat, and oh that fabulous glossy hair. Back then, the First Lady's fashion style was a breath of fresh air for the United States.

She continued to inspire the world until her passing in 1994. An entire generation of American women copied her style. Ladies all over the world wanted to dress like her, be her, and comb their hair like her.

Her understated elegance, European-chic, and sense of style still influence the way we dress today.

Jackie's fabulous beehives, bouffant, flirty bob flicks, and various fringe lengths were so chic and edgy, with her iconic hairstyles strongly influencing today's current hair trends. I personally feel that her hairstyles have been the greatest inspiration during my hair career. No matter the project, I continue to reference her when creating a mood board.

It's difficult to find a fashion designer who has not been inspired by her glamour or copied her signature fashion style in some way.

'Once you can express yourself, you can tell the world what you want from it... all the changes, good or evil, were first brought about by words.'

- JACQUELINE BOUVIER KENNEDY

Maybe you'll find your inspiration in music. Think Kiss, for their symbolic costumes, or Boy George, Freddie Mercury, or David Bowie, who immediately take you down memory lane and can offer incredible inspiration for your avant-garde directions. Also, Lil Nas X, Billy Porter, Billie Eilish, Rihanna, Madonna, or Lady Gaga have all combined their exceptional music talents and incredible fashion sensibilities. You can easily be energised by their thought-provoking musical genius.

While we're exploring inspiration, there are numerous influential fashion designers such as Alexander McQueen, Guo Pei, Iris van Herpen, Dame Vivienne Westwood, Coco Chanel, and Karl Lagerfeld to get you thinking. Explore their current collections and delve deep into their archives while taking into consideration colour, fashion, makeup, hair, and the creative directions that influenced them.

Dame Vivienne Westwood

This acclaimed English fashion designer was regarded as the Queen of Punk fashion. She first came to be noticed when she and Malcom McLaren opened their King's Road boutique and began to design clothing. Together they fuelled one another's creative vision influenced by punk culture.

   Safety pins, slashed jeans, exposed zippers, and raw controversial slogans were synonymous with their designs back then. Their contentious creations attracted members of the punk movement and various subcultures. With the evolution of time, Westwood seamlessly transitioned her extraordinary design skills to creating 19th century corsetry, hooped crinoline skirts using tartans, and plaids. She had exceptional tailoring skills that combined with her unique ability to drape and manipulate fabric into beautiful shapes and forms. She continues to inspire me with her incredible artistry many decades on.

> 'Intelligence is composed mostly of imagination, insight – things that have nothing to do with reason.'
>
> - DAME VIVIENNE WESTWOOD

Coco Chanel

Gabrielle Bonheur Chanel was born in France in 1883. A rebellious trailblazer, later known as Coco Chanel.

She was a prolific fashion creator, and ruled the Paris Haute Couture scene for six decades.

Her designs were fluid and androgynous, with a youthful ease.

Her original goal as a young fashion designer was to free women from the contrived corseted layers and petticoats of the past, and inspire women with a new approach to fashion in a way not expected at that time. She made black look chic, and clothing functional, minimalistic and exceptionally stylish.

Famed for the little black dress (LBD), her design aesthetically redefined fashionable women post World War One. Chanel is also known for that two-piece collarless suit which continues to evolve in the house of Chanel today.

Of her many memorable sayings, I identify most with this one:

> 'A girl should be two things… classy and fabulous.
> In order to be irreplaceable, one must always be different.'
> - COCO CHANEL

Alexander McQueen

When I'm asked who is my favourite fashion house, it's a close race between Alexander McQueen, Dolce & Gabbana, Westwood, or Moschino ... I love them all!

But Alexander McQueen is without doubt my all-time favourite. When I was lucky enough to visit his exhibition at the V&A museum in London in 2015, I still remember being moved to tears sitting amongst a treasure trove of his extraordinary designs and the legacy left from his lifetime of work.

I recall a quote that continues to resonate with me today. "You need to learn to construct, before you can deconstruct" – this quote is shared regularly with my students as it crosses over into the hair styling world. Learning to construct... perfecting the art of clean classical styling, before you deconstruct the hair into soft loose textured looks.

Alexander McQueen was one of the most celebrated designers of his generation. His exceptional technical ability, precise tailoring, and audacious original designs coupled with his historical narrative continued throughout his career and translated into his many collections. "I like to challenge history," he said in an interview. He will be forever my inspiration when researching for projects, and will be remembered as a designer of exceptional technical abilities.

'There comes a time in your life when you focus solely on what you believe is right, regardless of what everybody else is doing.'

– ALEXANDER McQUEEN

Floristry, hats, and art

Floral designers have a visionary aesthetic using flowers and foliage. Their innate ability to blend and combine colours, to mix soft and hard blooms and various textures, along with the ability to fabricate dramatic shapes is quite incredible to study. A few names to explore include Lauren Sellen, Azuma Makoto, and Melissa Richardson.

With regards to milliners, check out Phillip Treacy and Stephen Jones. They have inspired me continuously for shape, texture, and different hat constructions that can also be re-imagined into hair designs.

And you can also check out famous artists – here are a few to get you going: Antoni Gaudi, Andy Warhol, Salvador Dali, and Pablo Picasso. Explore the influence of art during different periods such as Pop Art, Cubism, Art Deco, Futurism, and Bauhaus to name just a few. Nothing is out of bounds, it's whatever energises you and gets the pulse racing.

Movies

Ok, let's talk movies and TV shows. It's quite impossible to know where to begin. It really depends on what direction you're thinking. A few to consider for starters are *Bridgerton, Downton Abbey, The Great Gatsby, Elizabeth, Marie Antoinette,* and *Jewelled Nights* – these are all fabulous fashion extravaganzas and provide perfect historical inspiration.

Casablanca, any Alfred Hitchcock movie, *Schindler's List, Breakfast at Tiffany's, Mad Men, Barbarella* for 1960s inspiration, *The Fifth Element* or even *Mad Max* – these are just a handful of suggestions that come to mind and are worth watching. I'm sure you've seen some fantastic movies that have also inspired you for various reasons during your own research.

Throughout history, hair has been worn in different styles, mainly determined either by culture, religion, social status, ethnicity, or fashion. When embarking on a new creative project, researching the history of hair can be extremely helpful to open up a new artistic direction. Google and Pinterest are great places to start this research.

My favourite hair artists and photographers

My suggestion list would not be complete without listing my favourite hair artists.

Alexandre' De Paris, Low Dicksum, Guido Palau, Sam McKnight, Eugene Souleiman, Julien d'Ys, Sylvestre Finold, Esteban Emmanuel, Laurent Philippon, X-Presion, Angelo Seminara, and Nicolas Jurnjack are just for starters!

There are always photographic images in my story boards. My favourite inspirational photographer at the moment is **Paolo Roversi**. His dreamlike ethereal images with diffused lighting offer a timeless classical vision.

Other notable favourites include Steven Meisel, Tim Walker, Irving Penn, Helmut Newton, Richard Avedon, and my favourite Australian hair photographer, Andrew O'Toole. Check them out!

Paolo Roversi

The thing that originally attracted me to the photography of Paolo Roversi was the dreamlike atmosphere, with soft lighting and beautiful emotion that his incredible images portray.

After initially being introduced to the work of this contemporary fashion and commercial photography master, I became obsessed with his unique trademark photography style.

I began researching in greater depth the 'how and why' of what set him apart from other great photographers of his time. I came to discover his love of shooting with large format Polaroid film, and there are claims that he brought the last lot of film available before it was discontinued. He was critical of most digital photography, and through his distinctive process, he perfected the art of creating striking classical images with a stunning ethereal expressive and emotional feel.

It's a given that one of his beautiful images will grace my mood board when preparing for a photo shoot, along with many other creative artists. A true visionary with passion for his craft, Paolo Roversi has become a global inspiration for photographers and fashion houses worldwide.

> 'I'm not the kind of photographer who always has a camera around his neck, always taking pictures of everything, with the fear of losing the moment. My life is full of pictures I didn't take, or that I just took with my mind because I wasn't fast enough with the camera. Maybe one day I'll write a book about the pictures I didn't take.'
> – PAOLO ROVERSI

Costume designers/stylists and makeup artists

Legendary costume designers Edith Head, Sandy Powell, Catherine Martin, Grace Coddington, and Ann Roth, to name just a few, are worth putting on the must-see list when researching fashion inspiration. These extraordinary minds are the greatest and most influential costume designers in film history.

And I can't forget to list my favourite makeup artists that are bound to get the heart rate pumping! Top of the class has to be Pat McGrath, Richard Taylor, Tom Pecheux, Charlotte Tilbury, Peter Philips, and a few Aussie favourites – Chereine Waddell, Nicole Thompson, and Kylie O'Toole.

Grace Coddington

One of my favourites, Grace Coddington's long illustrious career into the world of fashion began after winning a *Vogue* modelling competition. Unfortunately, her very successful modelling career was short-lived due to facial injuries sustained after a car accident.

Following on from this, she began working for *Vogue* as a junior writer, but she is most remembered as Creative Director at Large for American *Vogue*.

For 30 years she brought life to the pages of *Vogue* through her story telling, glamour, and cinema. Grace Coddington produced some of the most creative, complex, and extremely dramatic photoshoots and memorable imagery that has impacted the fashion, print and art world, symbolising her remarkable talent.

Rarely has one person personally made such a huge impact artistically on me. Flicking through pages of *Vogue* spellbound by the sheer brilliance of the images she created, or seeing the fabulous fashion on Sarah Jessica Parker in *Sex in the City*, I'm forever a diehard fan.

Ranking as one of the most influential fashion editors of our time, this woman's talents know no boundaries. And I continue to look back at her huge body of work as a reference point for my inspiration, as so many creatives and colleagues do so as well.

> *'Three rules of success in fashion: perseverance, dream a bit, and be passionate about it.'*
> – GRACE CODDINGTON

Architects

Another reference for creative influence is Architecture. Frank Lloyd Wright, Antoni Gaudi, Frank Gehry, and Zaha Hadid are all recognised as true masters of their craft. Architecture is the fabric of society – it influences, inspires, and shapes the environment.

In the past I used the *Guggenheim Museum Bilbao* as a catalyst for one of my collections. Google this museum and observe the overall spectacular shape, striking texture, along with the sculpture form. The undulating curves catching the light and high shine was the main reference that helped transition these details across to my hair designs.

Searching for new ideas begins with scouring the internet and looking at the original creator of your inspirational idea. The origin reason as to why it was created in the first place is always great underpinning knowledge to have. It gives you a base to grow your concept from, and it's always fun to explore the why. Here is a little more on one of my standout architectural icons:

Antoni Gaudi

A Spanish architect born in 1852, recognised as a pioneer and the greatest exponent of Catalan Modernism and Art Nouveau architecture. He was a visionary beyond his time.

His style of architecture was known for its distinctive geometrical designs and intricate avant-garde structures. He boldly used colours, textures, and embellishments that included porcelain tiles, intricate metal, wrought iron, and mosaics.

Gaudi's treasured masterpieces are evident throughout Barcelona where you can immerse yourself in the history and extreme splendour of his work. Viewed by millions, his most famous design is the Basilica de la Sagrada Família in Barcelona.

I personally find Antoni Gaudi's work incredibly inspirational, especially when creating avant-garde hair. Be it in the colour combinations, the unique shapes, or intricate textures, his work is worth exploring deeper when searching for that creative inspiration.

> *'Nothing is invented, for it's written in nature first.'*
> – ANTONI GAUDI

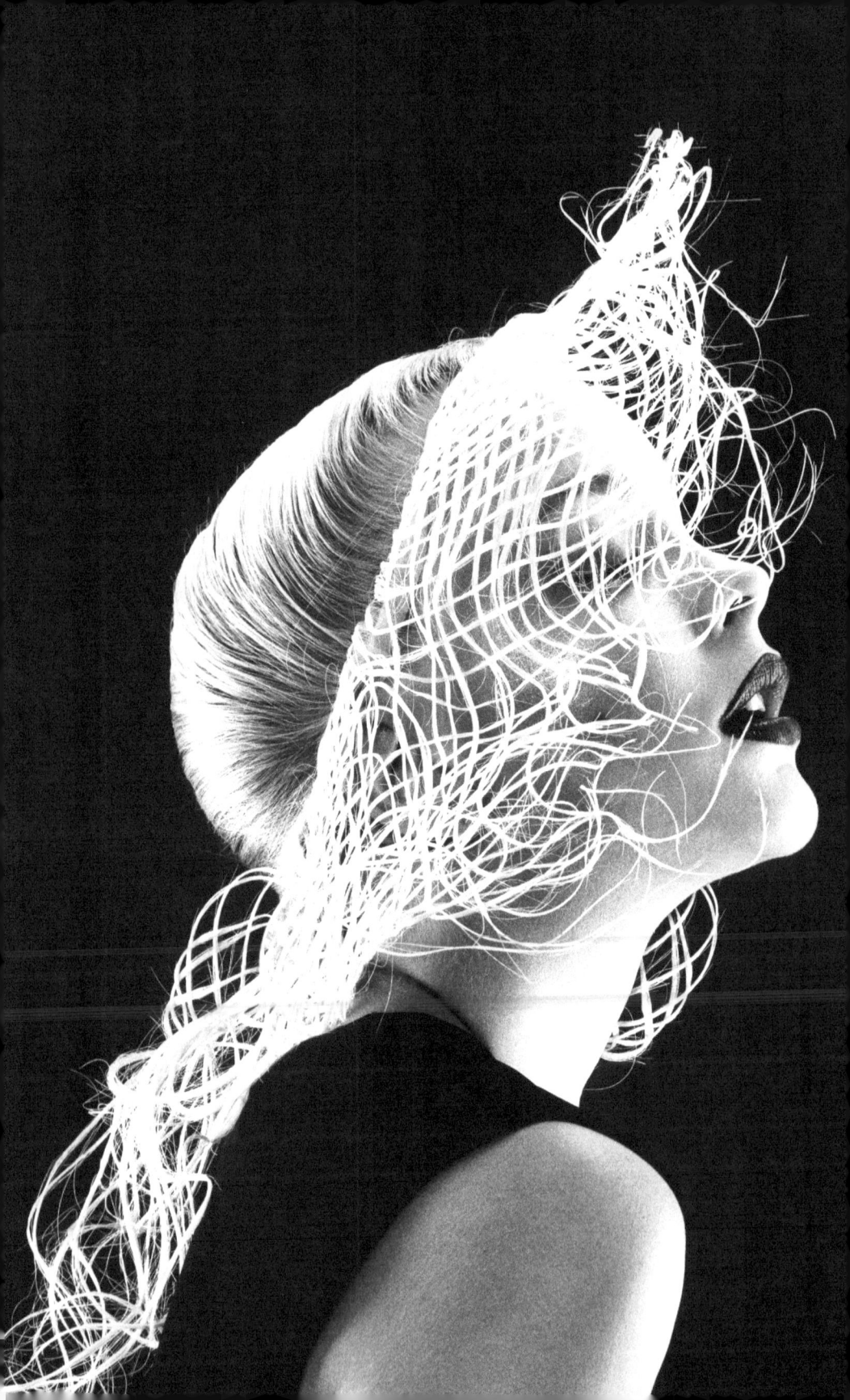

CHAPTER 14

THE CREATIVE PROCESS

'Dream big, what have you got to lose.'

– SHARON BLAIN

I'd like to now share thoughts on how inspiration and ideas are formed.

Hair styling is a creative artform that requires a unique idea, an inspirational concept, along with strong fundamental hair skills that come together to develop the visual design imagined.

So how is an idea formed and where does it come from? The dictionary states that an idea *'is a thought, a notion, and an awareness of a possible course of action.'*

Ideas can be for a design, shape, theme, or a solution. An idea sparks something that inspires and excites you.

Your thoughts, your vision, a dream, maybe a book or an experience – these all have the ability to evoke an emotion. Often your thoughts are about ideas that accumulate over a period of time. Ideas generally continue to evolve, creating a plan that is stored in the subconscious mind.

When the ideas finally mature, and when the mind and heart are working cohesively together, then the vision can fully evolve.

Tips on managing the creative process

For many years, I've carried a small A5 sketch/notebook everywhere I go. When travelling or in a quiet place, I seem to have the ability to visualise some great ideas. When my mind is free from distraction, especially social media, I'm surprised at how my ideas begin to accelerate and flow freely.

I have over 50 of these little books, and I love to sit and pore over their little gems, re-reading over and over again what I've written or sketched.

I have thousands of photos and screenshots of different ideas that have grabbed my attention and excite me. It could be fashion, hair, a painting, artwork… anything that catches my eye.

I strongly suggest that you always have a notebook handy to write down ideas as they come to mind, to draw a mind map using descriptive words about your ideas. Since we live in such fast-paced times where we are so visually stimulated, it's vital to capture the ideas and inspirations as they evolve, otherwise we can miss a golden opportunity. The more you write down and capture your ideas, the more you begin to feel a greater clarity, allowing the creative process to begin.

There are also some great apps available that will help to capture your creative process. It's paper versus digital, and really, it's what works easiest and best for you.

The Creative Brief

I've received many different types of briefs during my time in the industry. The most memorable was an 80-page extremely comprehensive brief for a new hair product launch. The detail was extensive, which really helped me in understanding the job, and I felt totally prepared for the shoot. Below is a list of what the brief involved:

- Overview of the company's history and direction
- Details of the new product being launched with the development phase and process
- Results of the market survey
- The target market
- The graphic design layouts from the advertising company for social, print, packaging, and signage
- Detail on font style, Pantone reports, packaging style, and brand guidelines
- Then it covered the key fashion, makeup, and hair trend forecasting

I must say I was overwhelmed in the beginning, but on the flip side, the depth of detail and information in this brief certainly helped me to nail the job. Since being exposed to this 'ultimate creative brief', it has taught me the importance of detail, and that the more effort that goes into the written brief, the better the result.

WHETHER IT'S A MOOD BOARD, VISION BOARD, CREATIVE BRIEF OR A STORYBOARD, THE MAIN PURPOSE IS TO PRODUCE AN EXCEPTIONAL CREATIVE PRODUCT.

Storyboard

There are different types of storyboards, and they are more commonly used for film, video, advertising, or movie productions. It's a visual graphic representation of a film sequence and breaks down the action into individual panels. It's created with a series of ordered drawings, with camera direction, dialogue, and other essential details. It sketches out how a video will unfold step by step.

    It's quite intriguing to see how the rows of individual boxes of stick figure sketches have the ability to map in sequential format and convey the vision of the producer. I learnt about storyboards and how to understand them during a movie I was involved in recently. It's considered the road map for all the teams – from hair, makeup, styling, props, and all the film crew involved in the production.

Vision board

The vision board is the exact visual representation of your creative goal. Simply put, it's a blueprint for an artistic project.

It's designed to keep everyone on track with strong direction for the project ahead. Generally, it's created electronically and then shared among the team to engage them in a robust discussion, cementing the desired result. The vision board ensures each individual is aware of what is required of them creatively and the role they play in the process. It eliminates any confusion and is vital for a positive outcome.

Mood board

For years master storytellers have used the mediums of mood and story boards to draw out their inspiration before executing an actual creative project. The versatility of these visual maps are used in all creative fields from designers, photographers, and hair and makeup for shoots.

A mood board is generally used to capture a cluster of sketches, inspirational images, fabric, and colour swatches, and it also allows creative ideas to be loosely organised. These images can cover many topics. Think of it like a brainstorming session with heaps of different ideas that capture the mood, emotion, aesthetic, composition, colour, and theme.

CHAPTER 15

MATERIAL LIST AND BUDGET

'Price is what you pay, value is what you get'

– WARREN BUFFET

When I started to develop my avant-garde pieces, I found so many different tools and materials that have been useful in developing them. They made the job easier and have become my 'tools of the trade' for artistic hair creations.

I studied floristry some years back and realised that the dry floral foam used for dried flower arrangements was light and great to use as a base for hair artistry. The variety of 18-32mm gauge wires were also very useful when creating different techniques that need wire to hold and secure.

Also, I have always been fascinated with hat making and realise that the materials used there were not visually dissimilar to hair. I began to blend hair and millinery fibres together and created some beautiful pieces.

I love these fibres as they are light, very mouldable, and simple to work with. The key message is 'keep it light' – it's so important to create pieces that will not be too heavy on the wearer's head. Hair is quite dense and will be heavy when too much is used. Abaca fibres are light to use when filling in a wire cage, and then adding hair as a veil over the top.

You'll see in upcoming pages I've compiled a long list including where to find the materials, equipment, and must-have tools that I like to have on hand when the creative process begins. Please keep this list handy so you can check out the items whenever the need arises.

Hopefully this list will be useful in helping you locate all the items you need to begin your journey to create stunning hair creations. I'm sure there are a whole host of other items not listed that you'll come across as you develop your skills and preferences.

One item I can't live without is a flat dense polystyrene board. When sourcing the board, make sure it's strong enough to take pins and not fall apart. These boards are great for creating intricate hairpieces. A good tip: wrap the pieces and the boards together using cling wrap as this holds them in place and stores everything safely.

MATERIALS USED FOR CREATIVE HAIR:

Millinery suppliers
- Face netting
- Double-sided stiff buckram

Craft stores online
- Handmade abaca fibre sheets
- Abaca Scrunch
- Tangle tuft sinamay scrunch fabric
- Mesh polyester fabric for cages
- *Solvy* plastic dissolvable fabric
- Polyester bridal net
- Synthetic faux fur long pile
- Clear nylon invisible thread
- Various types of curved metal needles, plastic sewing needles, extra-long needles
- T-Pins and glass headed pins
- Polystyrene flat boards
- Toothpicks and long metal skewers
- Polyester cotton core spun thread

Wig supplies
- Calico bald head short and long neck blocks
- Polystyrene head blocks
- Big plastic mesh padding shapes
- Wig tape and remover
- Wig glue and remover

Florist suppliers
- Florist black mesh wrap
- Artificial black floral foam blocks
- Different sized wires

Hardware stores
- Masking tape for temporary wig bases
- Floor sanding disc
- Black nylon fly screen wire
- Semi/gloss spray paint
- Pliers/wire cutters

Glues

- Hot glue gun
- Quick-dry adhesive
- Spray adhesive
- Spray glue
- Schwarzkopf Got2b Glued gel
- Spirit gum and spirit gum remover
- Wig glue and wig remover
- *Gafquat* liquid or gel

Wires

- Florist wire, from 16–32mm gauge
- Millinery wire for cages with a 16mm, 18mm, or 19mm gauge
- Jewellery wire with a 20mm gauge

Sharonblain.com

- Synthetic padding
- Elevate Pro Styler

Product suggestions

- Rhino Tough-Instant Gel Glue
- Evo Builders Paradise Working Spray
- Paul Mitchell Soft Sculpting Spray Gel
- Weightless shine spray

Hair Suggestions

- Synthetic jumbo hair braids
- Synthetic/human hair sewn hair wefts
- Tape-in wefts
- Hair toppers
- Wigs varying from top of the range hand-tied Swiss lace, to budget fully machine-made wigs
- False human hair fringes

Budget

When it comes to setting a budget, one important question to ask yourself…how much are you prepared to pay for a top-quality photography collection?

Over the years the amount of money I've spent to produce my photography collections has varied considerably. The price variant depends on the importance of the collection or how determined you are to take home the winner's trophy.

When it comes to shooting for an award, it's amazing how much money and time a hair artist is prepared to throw at a shoot in the name of winning.

Each year I create a new collection for my education program. These collections are generally styled around red carpet, bridal and more commercial hairdressing. I work with a very low budget and negotiate with all the team and models for the best prices. Even going so far as to do contra deals to keep the price down. I still believe the results of these collections are quite stunning, and it never ceases to amaze me how much you can save if you're prepared to put in the work to negotiate fees. A budget for creating marketing and social media assets generally comes in around $6,500–$8,000AUD all up.

Let's take a look at my **Abstract Collection** as an example of a lower-end budget shoot.

In the middle of the pandemic and during lockdowns, I felt totally starved of creative direction and lacking motivation, so I challenged myself to produce a new avant-garde collection for the Australian Hairdressing Awards.

LOWER-END BUDGET – MY ABSTRACT COLLECTION

Abstract was born from a collaboration with a digital animation specialist and fashion designer, Oscar Keene, where we explored what was possible to create together. Realising it would be impossible to do a shoot during lockdown with live models and makeup artists etc, this was the next best option. I believe it was the perfect partnership artistically, and also financially.

The creative process was quite unique – I've never met Oscar except via phone and email. Yet we both felt the creative collaboration and challenge would be a great opportunity to explore something special for us both.

I felt like I was working backwards in the beginning, as it started with him designing the fashion (which I had no say in), and then creating the incredible animated avatars.

Once the avatars were developed, the hair had to complement the clothing and angle for each one.

The challenge for me artistically, was to build the hair looks to work with the fashion in mind, whilst knowing the hair was to be stuck on bald shiny mannequin heads which I had hired – I had the added pressure of applying each piece of hair without damaging the surface.

I only needed to book my photographer for two hours, and we shot on a green screen background, sitting each mannequin on a milk crate.

Keeping the budget in mind, all the hairpieces were made from recycled materials, using pieces from other shoots – it's amazing how resourceful one becomes when needed!

The end result was definitely thought-provoking, and quite controversial, but I loved it – especially as the final cost was approximately $2,200AUD.

I'm still amazed at what can be achieved on a limited budget whist also becoming a finalist in the Avant-Garde category.

Abstract

HIGHER-END BUDGET – MY INFINITY COLLECTION

Infinity means never ending, evolving forever. My **Infinity Collection** was my biggest budget shoot, taking over six months of research and testing to get the hair to perform like fabric.

I set about challenging myself to produce a collection that pushed the boundaries that one would deem almost impossible to achieve with hair.

I wanted the hair to work in a way that was different than normal - for it to be more like hair fabric. I was inspired by unusual shapes and various textures, and each look related in some form to marine life, namely sea urchins, sea horses, coral, fishing nets, fish scales, and clams.

Getting the right hair texture to cut with a 3D cutter on the computer, took lots of trial and error. Experimenting with different types of glues and sprays, and learning the art of origami to fold the hair into different shapes, was relentless and exhausting, but riveting all at the same time.

I owe a depth of gratitude to Kate Robinson, a dear friend and fabulous graphic designer, who continued to experiment with different techniques and ideas up until the day of the shoot. The strong design elements were not only a challenge for Kate and I to create, but even today stylists continue to question me how some of the looks were achieved!

Throughout the process, there were constant team meetings, with lots of my sketches being rejected by Andrew O'Toole, the master photographer who shot the collection.

The pared back fashion styling, with lots of texture, sheen, and interesting lines, was the styling brief. The makeup was a nod to the movie, *Gods of Egypt*, using strong eyeliner in very different ways.

A simple grey background to avoid distracting away from the hair, with perfect lighting to bring the hair to life, was the brief for the photographer. Blonde and white hair was used to help show the intricate detailing in the different hairpieces.

This collection ended up being my most favourite, and also the most expensive costing upwards of $20,000 all up.

It's vital to build a strong relationship with a talented photography team whose work you trust and love working with. This way, you can call

Infinity

in favours when the budget is tight, and alternatively pay the current rates when you're able and want to shoot a high-end collection with all the bells and whistles.

A strong cohesive photographic team with passion for their craft takes years to cultivate. Having confidence in your team of choice is vital when delivering the ultimate photography results.

On the following page I've created an example of what a current pricing structure for a shoot in the Australian market would be. I'd expect it will vary from country to country, but this will give you a guide.

Keep in mind most professionals are happy to negotiate on their fees, but some are definitely not.

A little tip

I recommend sharing your ideas, storyboard, and brief with the team prior to discussing budgets. Once they're invested in your vision, you're more likely to get them on board, and they might be open to negotiate.

This list covers the approx. cost for the shoot in $AUD, bearing in mind this is just an estimate, and over time most costs will rise.

- Photographer $2,500–$10,000 per day
- Photographer Assistant $800–$1,500
- Retouching $250–$1,000 per image
- Videographer $1,500–$4,500 per day
- Studio hire $800–$4,000 per 8-hour day
  (Hiring of lights, backdrops, stands etc from $500)
- Prop hire $500–$3,000 depending on design
- Clothing Stylist $1,500–$3,500 per day
  (Sourcing clothing, returns, hire etc: $350 per model)
- Makeup Artist $1,000–$2,500
- Model $800–$2,500 per day with usage rights for 12 months
  (Additional charges might be charged for social media use)
- Wigs and Hairpieces per head $300–$3,500
- Hair Assistant $250–$500 per day
- Catering $20–$45 per head per day

CHAPTER 16

MY RENAISSANCE COLLECTION

'We learn from failure, not from success.'

– BRAM STOKER

It would be remiss of me not to walk you through my personal journey of shooting an awards collection. *The six images dotted throughout this chapter form this collection.*

Let me set the scene. It was that time again, awards season, and the moment for me to get into competition mode. I was a little overwhelmed with where to go with my ideas. My major issue was that in the previous year for the very first time, I'd won the *Hair Expo Best Photographic Collection of the Year* award with my *Infinity Collection*. To give you an idea of the importance of this win, my collection was voted number 1 out of some 350 photography collections entered that year!

So, I needed to come up with something bigger and better than ever before, no pressure!

My philosophy throughout life, especially when it comes to hair, is that if you can't create a better collection than the last one, then don't do it at all.

Chatting with colleagues about my dilemma, one suggested I check out the movie *Elizabeth* starring Cate Blanchett. Dare I say, I rented the video (you know, back in the day when you rented movies you wanted to watch on video!), and the rest is history.

After seeing the movie, I was immediately galvanised by the incredible hair, fashion, and makeup. It stole many hours of my time as I delved

into the historic references of that era. This deep dive opened a world of discovery into the life, the legends, and the myths of the time. I was like a dog with a bone, and I spent weeks and weeks reading, researching, and becoming immersed in Renaissance history.

This period was known as the *Golden Age,* and depending on your social class, there were different types of dress prohibited to be worn by law. The upper class wore more exquisite fabrics of silk, brocades, and velvets, with designs that were more restricted in movement and quite elaborate. The 'widow's peak' was considered beautiful and regal at the time, and the upper-class ladies plucked their hairlines to create its shape.

When Queen Elizabeth I came to the throne, she made red hair very fashionable. And here's a little trivia for you - saffron, cumin seeds, henna, and sulphur was used to create different hair colours resulting in various shades of gold, apricot, auburn, and reds that were worn by the nobility and aristocratic ladies of the era.

When analysing the hair shapes and decorative pieces of the time, I noticed a nod to a heart shape reference in the hair around the face, continuing the widow peak vibe.

A centre hair parting was popular, and the silhouette shape had width on either side of the head when the hair was worn up. Most hairstyles were adorned with precious jewels, gold, and pearls.

    I took my inspiration from this heart shape feature for the hair direction in my collection. In terms of makeup, the women used a lot of white, which explained the odd powdery white faces in many portraits of the time, with rouge pink cheeks for a touch of colour. I loved this makeup and felt it was important to reference the pale skin and rosy pink cheeks, but I decided to use this purely as inspiration for the makeup, giving it a more modern and futuristic feel.

    The elaborate fashion worn by the upper classes was unimaginable. I can't conceive of the amount of time it must have taken to dress with the laced-up corsets, petticoats, wire cages, and panniers panels that added width to the sides of skirts. Imagine adding these pieces, even before the top layers and gowns were put on. What would it have been like to move around, let alone sit down?

    This was further enhanced with starched ruffle collars on the neck, lavish gowns with plush fabrics like rich velvets and brocades, embellished with luxurious gold threads and jewellery. One can't help but be inspired by the grandeur this era presents.

    When settling on the direction for this collection, the most important thing for me was not to recreate the past, but to take some key elements from this era and push the direction into a more futuristic vibe.

    I approached this carefully with my creative brief:

Photography brief
- Close cropping from the waist/bust up.
- Dark background with strong bright lighting on the hair to pop the colour.

Fashion brief
- Starched collars.
- Luxury fabrics with a rich intense colour palette.
- Excessive embellishment at the neckline, due to the close cropping restricted to the upper body.

Makeup brief
- All models have pale coloured powder skin tone keeping with the Elizabethan era.
- No fake tan.
- Rose cheeks, subtle eye colour, and natural soft lips tones – less is more.
- Bleached eyebrows to give an alien look.

Hair brief

- Bright warm hair colours.
- All 6 looks to have a variation of tones ranging from golden blonde, yellow, apricot, rich reds, through to deep plum.
- Working with various nuances including a widow's peak, centre parting, and width at the sides.
- A mix of 3 styling and 3 precision haircut photos. The cuts featured fringes with variations on the widow's peak.
- Different styling techniques including basket weaving, looped texture, and braiding, all with a forward-thinking direction.

By walking you through this brief history lesson, my goal was to share insight into how my **Renaissance Collection** evolved. Once I established the direction for the shoot and the inspiration behind it, the shoot itself naturally evolved from that point forward. Keeping to the brief is the key to success. It is essentially your blueprint, the architectural plan you can't live without!

Pro tip: While creating the hair looks, always ask yourself, is this idea in keeping with the creative brief, or have I introduced different elements that don't work with the concept? Keeping on track and not shifting away from the brief is by far the hardest thing to do as stylists. We have so many ideas floating around in our heads and we want to use them all!

Being prepared to drop a great hair idea takes a lot of courage, but if it doesn't fit the brief, you need to make the call.

The final step was to brief the team involved. Selling the vision and bringing them on board with the concept is so important. You want everyone 'singing from the same song book' so to speak. The team need to be invested in both your ideas, and your plan of how to get there.

With a cohesive team, nothing is left to chance and all the magic happens.

And speaking of magic ... I hope you've taken away a huge dose of styling magic in the form of the tried, tested, and true!

From the massive highs to the epic fails of over 50 years, I've come to be the *Go-To Queen of Styling* all around the world, and now I've passed some of that along to you.

All that's left is for you to *be* THE CONFIDENT STYLIST.

Wishing you all the very best,

P.S. and remember ... style never goes out of fashion!

IMAGE CREDITS

Front cover
Hair: Sharon Blain
Photographer: Kylie Coutts
Styling: Emma Cotterill
Makeup: Julie Elton

Page 3
Hair: Sharon Blain
Image courtesy of *Culture Magazine* photo shoot

Page 4
Hair Directors: Sharon Blain & Peter Gray
Hair Team: Sharon Blain's New York Student Photographic Team, 2017
Photographer: Anthony Friend
Stylist: Sabine Feuilloley
Makeup: Marla Belt

Page 6
Hair: Sharon Blain
Photographer: Israel Rivera
Stylist: Emma Cotterill
Makeup: Rachel Montgomery

Page 8
Hair: Sharon Blain
Photographer: James Demitri
Stylist: Kimberley Kessler
Makeup: Helen Samaryan

Page 10 & 16
Hair: Sharon Blain
Photographer: Stephan Ziehen
Stylist: Ingo Nahrwold
Makeup: Denise Grundmann

Page 17, 19 & 20
Photographer/Hair: Sharon Blain

Page 22
Hair: Sharon Blain
Photographer: Milos Mlynarik
Design and Digital Avatar: Oscar Keene

Page 23, 24, 25 & 26
Photographer/Hair: Sharon Blain

Page 28
Hair: Sharon Blain
Photographer: David Mannah
Stylist: Emma Cotterill
Makeup: Chereine Waddell

Page 31
Hair: Sharon Blain
Photographer: Anthony Friend
Stylist: Sabine Feuilloley
Makeup: Marla Belt
Floral design: Flourish Flower Merchants

Page 32, 34 & 35
Hair: Sharon Blain
Photographer: Milos Mlynarik
Stylists: Amber Leigh & Madelaine Caldwell
Makeup: Chereine Waddell

Page 37, 38, 39, 40, 41 & 42
Photographer/Hair: Sharon Blain

Page 48
Hair: Sharon Blain
Photographer: Ian Golding
Stylist: Olga Tamara
Makeup: Julie Elton

Page 52 & 53
Hair: Sharon Blain
Photographer: David Mannah
Stylist: Emma Cotterill
Makeup: Chereine Waddell

Page 57
Hair: Sharon Blain
Photographer: Ian Golding
Makeup: Julie Elton

Page 64, 85, 87, 90, 113 & 129
Hair: Sharon Blain
Photographer: James Demitri
Stylist: Britt McCamey
Makeup: Memo Gallard

Page 69
Elevate Pro Styler available at www.elevateprohair.com

Page 76
Image courtesy of Eco Ocean Haircare

Page 93, 95, 96, 97 & 98
Sketch Artist: Karina Siam Jimenez

Page 100 & 110
Hair: Sharon Blain
Photographer: Monica Buscarino
Stylist: Courtney Humphreys
Makeup: Matt Hornby

Page 104, 107, 108 & 109
Hair: Sharon Blain
Photographer: Sam Ansari,
Phao Photography

Page 114, 115, 116, 117 & 118
Hair: Sharon Blain
Photographer: Sam Ansari,
Phao Photography

Page 120
Hair: Sharon Blain
Photographer: Milos Mlynarik
Designer: Breeanna Maree
Stylists: Amber Leigh & Madelaine Caldwell
Makeup: Chereine Waddell

Page 123, 124, 125, 126, 127 & 128
Hair: Sharon Blain
Photographer: Sam Ansari,
Phao Photography

Page 125 & 126
Hair: Sharon Blain
Photographer: Ian Golding
Stylist: Lydia-Jane Saunders
Makeup: Susan Markovic

Page 130
Hair/Styling: Sharon Blain
Photographer: Ian Golding
Makeup: Julie Theodosis

Page 132, 136, 137, 138 (bottom left image) & 139
Hair: Sharon Blain
Photographer: Sam Ansari,
Phao Photography

Page 138
Image at top left of page Courtesy of GHD

Page 140
Hair: Sharon Blain
Photographer: Israel Rivera
Stylist: Emma Cotterill
Makeup: Rachel Montgomery

Pages 143, 144, 145, 146, 147, 148, 151, 153, 154, 155, 156, 157 (top right image) & 159
Hair: Sharon Blain
Photographer: Sam Ansari,
Phao Photography

Page 149
Padding shapes available at
www.sharonblain.com

Page 157
Photographer/Hair: Sharon Blain
(3 ponytail images)

Page 160
Hair: Sharon Blain
Photographer: Ian Golding

Page 163
Hair: Sharon Blain
Photographer: Ian Golding
Stylist: Craig Braybrook
Makeup: Memo Gallard

Page 165
Hair: Sharon Blain
Photographer: James Demitri
Stylist: Kimberley Kessler
Makeup: Helen Samaryan

Page 166
Hair: Sharon Blain
Photographer: Anthony Friend
Stylist: Sabine Feuilloley
Makeup: Marla Belt

Page 168
Hair: Sharon Blain
Photographer: Ian Golding
Stylist: Lydia-Jane Saunders
Makeup: Susan Markovic

Page 169 & 170
Hair: Sharon Blain
Image courtesy of *Modern Hair + Beauty Magazine*, Wildlife Publication

Page 171
Hair: Sharon Blain
Photographer: Ian Golding
Stylist: Olga Tamara
Makeup: Julie Elton

Page 172
Hair: Sharon Blain
Photographer: Ian Golding
Makeup: Julie Elton

Page 173
Hair: Sharon Blain
Photographer: Milos Mlynarik
Stylists: Amber Leigh & Madelaine Caldwell
Makeup: Chereine Waddell

Page 174
Hair: Sharon Blain
Photographer: Kylie Coutts
Stylist: Emma Cotterill
Makeup: Julie Elton

Page 190
Hair: Sharon Blain
Image courtesy of
Goldwell Colorance campaign
Photographer: Stephan Ziehen
Colourist: Roch Lemay

Page 192, 203, 210 & 213
Hair: Sharon Blain
Photographer: Andrew O'Toole
Stylist: Emily Sue Yee
Makeup: Rachel Montgomery

Page 200
Hair: Sharon Blain
Photographer: Anthony Friend
Stylist: Sabine Feuilloley
Makeup: Marla Belt

Page 208
Hair: Sharon Blain
Photographer: Milos Mlynarik
Design and Digital Avatar: Oscar Keene

Page 214, 216, 217, 218, 219 & 220
Hair: Sharon Blain
Photographer: Kylie Coutts
Stylist: Emma Cotterill
Makeup: Margaret Ashton
Colourist: Ashley Carothers-Swan

Back Cover
Photographer: Amie Baines @amiebaines
Image courtesy of @bonvivant2137

ACKNOWLEDGEMENTS

This book would not be possible if it wasn't for the encouragement of so many industry friends and colleagues. For all the long hairstylists who urged me to put pen to paper and share my knowledge about styling in print, thank you all for the continuing support.

Linda Cappa, thank you for your energetic and inexhaustible dedication to researching information, and your incredible enthusiasm writing day and night to deliver some fantastic information to help me in building the content.

A huge thank you to the incredibly talented hairstylist and artist Karina Sian Jimenez who I had the absolute pleasure to meet in Peru, for creating the beautiful pencil braiding images in Chapter 6.

Aili Puss, a number one talented creative and the most amazing hair artist from Estonia. Your hair knowledge, hair skills, and enthusiasm for the craft is extraordinary. Thank you for the incredible contribution you have made to hair education, and to the Sharon Blain Education brand, and for being a dear friend.

Thank you, Clare Rabbit from Flourish Flower Merchant in Sydney, for your beautiful floral images. You are one talented florist and a beautiful person.

Elli Julia, I'm so honoured to have you on my team your dedication, welcome advice, kindness, help, and articulate proofing skills are next level.

Thank you, Jessie from Eco Ocean Hair, for your help with the photos of your fab hair ties.

A huge thank you to all my beautiful models, makeup artists, fashion stylists, and the best photographers in the business, for creating the most spectacular photography images scattered throughout this book.

Not to forget all the hair assistants who I have had the pleasure to work with over the many years. Too many to name, but you know who you are. My hair assistants are the best in the world, and have worked with me for years. Thanks for handing up thousands of pins, for unpacking, and packing down my kits, and for being brave enough to give your constructive feedback on my creations. Thank you also for keeping my styling on-trend.

Thank you, Vanessa, Carley and Angie, who have been part of my team for many years and always have my back and for your tireless devotion. I could not think of a better team to be on my journey with me, and I could not have achieved it without you. I appreciate you for always agreeing with the all the wild ideas I dream up, and for helping bring them to life.

Finally, Rick, my partner for believing in me, and my amazing children and grandchildren who head up the fan club – love you all.

www.ingramcontent.com/pod-product-compliance
Lightning Source LLC
Chambersburg PA
CBHW041429300426
44114CB00002B/11